What Readers Are Saying

I recommend *A Place of Quiet Rest* to everybody who desires a deeper relationship God. It literally changed my life and my whole perspective on how I relate to the Lord on a personal level. I still refer to that book and will be reading it again.

I've been saved for almost twenty-two years, and this book has been such a refreshing reminder of how much I need God and how much He longs to spend time with me.

As a twenty-nine-year-old mother of three, *A Place of Quiet Rest* has had a huge impact on my life. I regret to say that I started this study with dread. "You mean I have to get up every morning and set aside time with the Lord?" I'm embarrassed now that I ever felt that way. True, it was a struggle the first few days but after that I began to have a hunger to know His Word. Now, I never want to stop learning, and I look forward every morning to my cup of coffee and time with my Lord. Thank you for igniting a fire inside of me that I only regret didn't start earlier in my life. Your book has been motivation for me to seek the Lord and spend time getting to know Him.

I read the entire book this week. It is one of the best things I have ever read on having an intimate relationship with God.

I purchased *A Place of Quiet R*
read it myself first. I could not
many additional copies for gift

What a challenging book to this pastor. Thank you. My personal devotions with the Lord, as well as my preaching, have benefited.

Your book took my time of devotion to new depths and new insight, helping the Word stay with me during the day. I can recommend this book to every believer, whether they have a good relationship with the Lord or struggle through their devotional times.

A Place of Quiet Rest

FINDING INTIMACY WITH
GOD THROUGH A DAILY
DEVOTIONAL LIFE

Nancy DeMoss Wolgemuth

MOODY PUBLISHERS
CHICAGO

© 2000, 2025
by Revived Hearts Foundation

All rights reserved. No part of this book may be reproduced in any form without permission in writing from the publisher, except in the case of brief quotations embodied in critical articles or reviews.

Unless otherwise indicated, Scripture quotations are from the ESV® Bible (The Holy Bible, English Standard Version®), © 2001 by Crossway, a publishing ministry of Good News Publishers. ESV Text Edition: 2025. The ESV text may not be quoted in any publication made available to the public by a Creative Commons license. The ESV may not be translated in whole or in part into any other language. Used by permission. All rights reserved.

Scripture quotations marked csb have been taken from the Christian Standard Bible,® Copyright © 2017 by Holman Bible Publishers. Used by permission. Christian Standard Bible® and CSB® are federally registered trademarks of Holman Bible Publishers.

Scripture quotations marked nasb are taken from the New American Standard Bible, Copyright © 1960, 1962, 1963, 1968, 1971, 1972, 1973, 1975, 1977, 1995 by The Lockman Foundation. Used by permission. All rights reserved. lockman.org.

Scripture quotations marked niv are taken from the Holy Bible, New International Version®, NIV®. Copyright © 1973, 1978, 1984, 2011 by Biblica, Inc.™ Used by permission of Zondervan. All rights reserved worldwide. www.zondervan.com. The "NIV" and "New International Version" are trademarks registered in the United States Patent and Trademark Office by Biblica, Inc.™

Scripture quotations marked nkjv are from the New King James Version. Copyright © 1982 by Thomas Nelson. Used by permission. All rights reserved.

Scripture quotations marked tlb are from The Living Bible copyright © 1971 by Tyndale House Foundation. Used by permission of Tyndale House Publishers Inc., Carol Stream, Illinois 60188. All rights reserved.

Scripture quotations marked kjv are from the King James Version.

Italics in Scripture references indicate author emphasis.

Names and details in some illustrations have been changed to protect individuals' privacy. Some of the correspondence cited has been edited for style and sense.

Published in association with the literary agency of Wolgemuth & Wilson.

Edited by Anne Christian Buchanan
Interior design: Kaylee Lockenour Dunn
Cover design: Brittany Schrock

ISBN: 978-0-8024-6642-6

We hope you enjoy this book from Moody Publishers. Our goal is to provide high-quality, thought-provoking books and products that connect truth to your real needs and challenges. For more information on other books and products written and produced from a biblical perspective, go to www.moodypublishers.com or write to:

Moody Publishers
820 N. LaSalle Boulevard
Chicago, IL 60610

1 3 5 7 9 10 8 6 4 2

Printed in Colombia

To my beloved Lord Jesus.

You are "Chief among ten thousand"
and "altogether lovely."
"The companions listen for your voice—
Let me hear it!"[1]

Jesus, Thou Joy of loving hearts,
Thou Fount of life, Thou Light of men,
From the best bliss that earth imparts,
We turn unfilled to Thee again.
We taste Thee, O Thou living Bread,
And long to feast upon Thee still;
We drink of Thee, the Fountain-head,
And thirst our souls from Thee to fill.

Bernard of Clairvaux, tr. Ray Palmer

CONTENTS

Preface to the 25th Anniversary Edition   9
Foreword: Before You Begin (by Joni Eareckson Tada)   11
From My Heart to Yours   13

Part One
The Priority of a Devotional Life

Chapter 1 A Day in the Life of the Lord   23
Chapter 2 Made for Intimacy   35

Part Two
The Purpose of a Devotional Life

Chapter 3 The Inner Life   51
Chapter 4 The Outer Walk   69

Part Three
The Pattern of a Devotional Life

Chapter 5 Getting Started   91

Part Four
The Problems of a Devotional Life

Chapter 6 "The Hard Thing for Me Is . . ."   111

Part Five
The Practice of a Devotional Life

SECTION 1: Receiving His Word

Chapter 7 The Wonder of the Word	137
Chapter 8 Getting into the Word	157
Chapter 9 Getting the Word into You	179

SECTION 2: Responding to His Word

Chapter 10 The Perfume of Praise	209
Chapter 11 The Privilege of Prayer	235

Part Six
The Product of a Devotional Life

Chapter 12 Cultivating the Garden of the Heart	257
Where to from Here? A 30-Day Challenge	273
Appendix: Recommended Devotional Books	277
Notes	279
Thank You	285
About the Author	287

Preface to the 25th Anniversary Edition

I've often said that if I could share just one message, it would be on the value and importance of a personal devotional life.

For sure, there are other vital truths that need to be communicated—I've addressed many of these over the course of decades of ministry. But I've always believed that the most helpful thing I could do for the women I serve is to get them into Scripture for themselves. That's because I'm convinced that if you and I are consistently getting to know God and His ways through His Word, He will show us everything we need to know in order to deal with our most thorny, perplexing problems and to live godly, fruitful, blessed lives.

> *If I could share just one message, it would be on the value and importance of a personal devotional life.*

So in 1998 when the team at Moody Publishers asked to

meet with me about the possibility of my writing a book, this is the topic that was on my heart.

For years, I had looked for a resource I could recommend to people who wanted to learn how to have a daily quiet time. I had read and benefited personally from many wonderful devotional books, but couldn't find a book that explained how to actually develop a personal devotional habit. It was to help meet this need that I was prompted to write what became my first book—the one you hold in your hands.

And what a great encouragement it has been, in the twenty-five years since its release, to see how God has used this message to draw readers into a more intimate relationship with Himself. My prayer is that this updated edition will encourage a new generation to experience the priceless treasure of seeking and savoring the Word of God and the God of the Word, above all else.

As you read this book, you should know that my desire is not just for you to learn more about a devotional life, but for this practice to become a way of life. That's why, when you get to the end, I'm going to invite you to take a 30-day challenge as a next step. (You'll find it on page 277, if you'd like to take a sneak peek. And, of course, you can start the challenge anytime you wish, even before you finish this book.)

If you'll follow through on this monthlong exercise, I believe you'll want to repeat it again and again. My hope and prayer is that as a result, you will enjoy an ever-increasing measure of the sweet fruit of knowing and loving our heavenly Father and His Son, Jesus Christ.

Nancy DeMoss Wolgemuth
September 2025

Foreword

Devotion to the Lord Jesus. We all desire it.
When it comes to drawing close to God, every Christian wants to be plunged under the waterfall of His joy. We want to get our hearts beating in rhythm with His. If we're sad, we want His smile. If we're lost, we want Him to find us. "Lord, embrace me with a passion that seizes and melts me into a union with You that can never be broken. Part the heavens and come down," we pray; "throw open the door of my heart and take possession."

Our Christian instincts call for this. It's getting there that's the struggle.

How do we get started? Flip open the Bible and "let the Spirit lead"? Study a topic? Memorize a chapter? Surround ourselves with commentaries and Bible dictionaries? (We want to do this right!) A carefully structured quiet time with the Lord is good, but a growing life of devotion to the Savior is more—much more—than "Do A, B, or C, and you will know Him better."

Personal relationships don't work that way, certainly not when it comes to God. Growing closer to someone—God or anybody—means pressing hearts together. Learning how to communicate. Finding joy in each other. Searching out the other's soul. A strong relationship is the weaving together of many shared experiences, some of which are serendipitous and off-the-cuff, others of which are structured and well-defined. Such things make for intimacy. Disciplining ourselves to spend regular time with someone, even with God, can be regulated, but not the intimacy itself.

A Place of Quiet Rest is a guide into that intimacy. Rather than a how-to book, Nancy DeMoss Wolgemuth provides for you an excellent road map: a guide using Scripture, testimonies, poems, counsel, and wisdom to help you know God and be known. *A Place of Quiet Rest* is anything but a mechanistic approach to cultivating a devotional life with the Lord Jesus; it is a gentle yet clear nudge on every page, a pointing-in-the-right-direction in every chapter. It is a book that will help you encounter God as you push past the regimen to the place where you can embrace the Savior in a natural—no, a *supernatural* way.

And what will happen when you, in turn, embrace God with a passion that seizes and melts you into sweet union with Him? How will you be affected as you follow the guides in *A Place of Quiet Rest*? As a saint of old once said, your joy will be fervent but not feverish. You will be energetic but not excitable. You will be speedy in doing things, but not hasty. Prudent, but not selfish. Resolute and fearless, but not rash. You will have joy without a lot of parade and noise. Your soul will be serene, yet people all around you will feel the influence of God.

It's what devotion to Jesus looks like on you.

Want it? Rather, do you want *Him*? You hold in your hands a splendid guide.

Joni Eareckson Tada

From My Heart to Yours

This is not a book written by an expert. Rather, it is written by a woman in process—a woman on a pilgrimage to know God.

That journey began months before I was born, as my parents dedicated me to the Lord and purposed to teach me (and the six other children who would follow) the Word and ways of God.

Much as a greenhouse is designed to nurture young plants and protect them from forces that might damage their tender roots, our parents sought to create in our home a climate that was conducive to spiritual growth, where we were nurtured in the Word and ways of God and sheltered from unwholesome or dangerous influences.

The Spirit used the spiritual care of those earliest years to cultivate the soil of my heart, to make it tender and responsive to His wooing and to make me aware of my need for a Savior. My first conscious memory, in fact, is of the afternoon of May 14, 1963, when at the age of four I gave my heart to Christ. In that moment God planted within me a seed—the seed of eternal life—and placed within me a new life—the life of His Son, Jesus.

Until that day, according to God's Word, I was "dead in... trespasses and sin" (Eph. 2:1)—I had no connection to the God of the universe. But at that moment, through repentance and faith in Jesus Christ, I became alive.

It's not hard to tell that a newborn baby is alive—she breathes, her heart beats, she gets hungry and thirsty, she grows, she communicates, she cries. And so my spiritual birth was accompanied by signs of spiritual life—a capacity and a longing to know God, a heart that beats and cries after God.

At the time, I had little comprehension of the fact that God is the supreme Lover who desires intimacy with His creatures. And I certainly had little awareness of the incredible price He had paid to make it possible for me to live in union and communion with Him.

All I knew was that I needed Him, that He wanted me, and that Jesus was the One who made it possible for us to have that relationship.

Now, looking back, I can see that what took place that day was the starting point of a relationship—a longing in my heart, corresponding to the longing in His heart, to know Him, to walk with Him, to enjoy fellowship with Him, and to share our lives together in an eternal love relationship. And early in my Christian life, I learned about one of the practical means to cultivate such a relationship with God. It had to do with something my earthly father practiced daily—something he called "devotions."

Each morning, in the midst of an extremely active and busy household and with the demands of growing a successful business, he managed to spend an hour or more alone with the Lord.

I don't recall ever actually being with him during those times—though I did frequently see him reading his Bible. But somehow we all knew that this time in the Word and prayer was more important to him than any other activity of his day. And as I got older, I learned something of how it had come to be such an indispensable part of his life.

During his teenage and young adult years, in search of thrills, my father became addicted to gambling, adopting a freewheeling lifestyle that destroyed any sense of values he might have had, and caused no little heartache to his parents. He was not looking for God—the Scripture indicates that there is no one who seeks after God—but the "Hound of heaven"[1] was pursuing him. And one night while in his midtwenties, having made a mess of his life, he came under the preaching of the gospel. He was converted and never looked back.

Early in his Christian life, my father was challenged to give the first part of every day to the Lord in the Word and in prayer. From that day until the day he went to heaven twenty-eight years later, *he never missed a single day* of this devotional practice. Nothing was more important to him than growing in his relationship with the Lord, and he believed strongly that nothing was more essential to maintaining that relationship than a daily time alone with the Lord.

Daily devotions were not something my parents ever forced on us, but the influence of my dad's example and training in this area was profound. Although he has been with the Lord since 1979, the image of a dad on his knees before the Lord (I don't know how many kneeling pads he wore out over the years) is indelibly etched on my mind and heart.

In God's kindness, when I was fifty-seven, never having been married, He brought a widower named Robert Wolgemuth into my life. I soon learned that, like my dad, this man knew and loved God's Word. And since the death of his first wife, Bobbie, Robert had become even more purposeful about starting each day in the Word and prayer, no matter what else was on the docket for the day. It was from Robert that I first heard a challenging phrase he had picked up from his late wife: "The Throne before the phone"—something Robert has modeled consistently to me.

Although I have made a practice since earliest childhood of beginning my day with the Lord, this discipline has not always come easily for me. As much as I value and need it, I have often struggled to make it a consistent reality. I have battled my flesh, which loves to sleep, is easily distracted, and does not like to sit still and be quiet. I have battled interruptions—many of my own making—and a never-ending to-do list.

> Although I have made a practice since earliest childhood of beginning my day with the Lord, this discipline has not always come easily for me.

There have been mornings when I've allowed my pillow, my phone, or an overflowing inbox to win out and have ended up spending only a few hurried moments with the Lord—even as I was writing this book on the subject! At times, I have missed out altogether on spending time alone with Him.

But I have come to believe with all my heart that this is something worth fighting for. The enemy of my soul knows if he can win this battle, he will be able to defeat me in other areas of my life. He hates God, and he works tirelessly to convince us that we can operate on our own, independently of our Maker. He's well aware that if we take that path, we will end up spiritually defeated, frustrated, barren, and fruitless. Worse, we will end up doubting God and His goodness, in bondage to our flesh, and resisting His will.

Over the years, I've discovered another, even more important, reason to guard this time alone with the Lord. I have come to see practicing "devotions" less as an obligation of the Christian life and more as an incredible opportunity to know the God of the universe. He has issued to you and me an invitation to draw near to Him and experience an intimate love relationship with Him. So for me (most days) "devotions" have become not so much a *duty* as a *delight*—an awesome privilege to share sweet union and communion with the Bridegroom of my soul.

> I have come to see practicing 'devotions' less as an obligation of the Christian life and more as an incredible opportunity to know the God of the universe.

Yet, I'm convinced that few subjects evoke such feelings of guilt, failure, and frustration among believers as the matter of "daily devotions."

Of those believers who do have some sort of devotional life, many—perhaps a majority—approach this time with the sense that it is something they *ought* to do. Others have tried and failed so many times they are tempted to give up—or they already have. Still others have never even started and have no idea what they are missing.

Then there are those whose lives bear the sweet, rich fruit of meeting with God on a consistent basis. I've been blessed to know a number of these people over the years, and the fragrance of their lives has deepened my own longing to know God.

One of those is a dear, longtime friend who I have watched weather seemingly endless storms of life with unshakable courage, grace, and peace. Anyone who knows Kimberly know the "secret."

As a teen, she experienced several years of fits and starts with a daily devotional life. Then, when she was a young pastor's wife, the Lord showed her the hypocrisy of trying to "do ministry" without first taking time to meet with Him. He brought her to make a commitment to start her day by seeking the Lord in His Word and prayer. She remembers thinking,

> With all the things that filled the hours of my day, could I not squeeze in at least a bit of time in God's Word each day? Could I not set that as my most important priority? Then it hit me that, just as I had made a vow to my husband to be faithful to him in marriage, surely I could make a similar vow to my Savior—to at least begin my day communicating with Him, seeking Him, and hearing from Him in His Word.

Kimberly acknowledges that it was hard to get started. But now, more than thirty years later, she says:

> That was the beginning of the greatest adventure I could ever experience on this side of eternity. My time with my Savior each morning is the most precious portion of each day. I've never regretted for a moment making that vow.
>
> Little did I know how very much I would need the daily consistency of that established habit *before* I reached the challenges of interrupted mornings with mothering little ones, *before* the challenging years of parenting teens while serving in a church

with complex problems, and *long before* extended seasons of hospital vigils and caregiving (first with my father, and later with both my mom and husband).

Life here is punctuated by brokenness, trauma, sorrow, and tragedy. That's the nature of living in a world under the curse (Rom. 8:20–22). But, through much loss and difficulty, spending the first portion of the day in God's Word, seeking His heart, has been my stability. Staying tethered to His Word provides me with wisdom beyond myself; guidance for each day's events, responses, and decisions; and joy that is indescribable as I get to know Him more and more intimately.

His Spirit uses His Word to open my eyes to hidden sin, blind spots, and areas of my life where I need to grow. He convicts me and leads me. In those first moments of the day, He prepares me for the rest of the day—setting my heart for the course He has planned for me. He knows what the day will hold—whether tragedy or joy—and spending time alone with Him prepares me for that.

Time in His Word leads me in how to intercede for others. Scripture shapes and informs my prayer life. My prayers become entwined with His Word.

Over the course of these years, I've come to know His character and have an intimacy with Him that is the gift I treasure most, more than anything that this world might offer. Truly there is no greater privilege than to know Him.

If you are a child of God, I believe there is within you something that will never be satisfied with anything less than sweet, intimate fellowship with your Creator, Redeemer, and heavenly Father. Until you see Him face-to-face, you will never cease to hunger and thirst to know Him more. Kimberly's example has increased that longing in my own soul. I hope it has done the same for you.

Jesus said, "If anyone thirsts, let him come to me and drink" (John 7:37). This is a book for thirsty souls. It is an invitation to come to *Him*—not to another program, another thing to add to your to-do list, another requirement—but to Jesus, the Source of all Life. Come to Him and drink. Drink deeply. Keep on drinking. Let Him quench your thirst. And then watch as rivers of living water flow out through you to quench the thirst of those around you.

PART ONE

The Priority of a Devotional Life

*One thing I have desired
of the L*ORD*, that will I seek.*
PS. 27:4 NKJV

The more I think of and pray about the state of religion in this country, and all over the world, the deeper my conviction becomes that the low state of the spiritual life of Christians is due to the fact that they do not realize that the aim and object of conversion is to bring the soul even here on earth to a daily fellowship with the Father in heaven.

When once this truth has been accepted, the believer will perceive how indispensable it is to the spiritual life of a Christian to take time each day with God's Word and in prayer, to wait upon God for His presence and love to be revealed.

ANDREW MURRAY

CHAPTER 1

A Day in the Life of the Lord

Often, while leading a women's conference, I have invited the attendees to write down why they've come and what they hope God will do in their lives during our time together. "Where does God find you as we start this weekend?" I ask.

In one instance, as I read the responses, I was amazed at how many of them sounded alike. Here's a sampling of what those women expressed:

- *"I feel I'm out of control sometimes with so many pressures."*
- *"I face too much stress and responsibility."*
- *"I need God to show me how to cope with the stresses at this moment."*
- *"I feel like I'm torn in all directions. I want God to show me how to manage my different 'hats' of teacher, mother, wife, and daughter successfully and still have time for church work and 'me.'"*

- *"I need to stop worrying about everything. I try not to, and I know I shouldn't, but worries that I conjure up even disturb my sleep and dreams."*
- *"I've given myself up to service for about twenty-four months, and I feel a need to slow myself down and renew myself, but life gets real hectic."*
- *"With a new baby, I need to find the Lord's peace and rest—physically and emotionally."*
- *"I often get overly busy and find my day gone without having done the things I most wanted to do."*
- *"I am a single person by divorce, and I really am tired."*
- *"I've left a whirlwind at home and need a renewed spirit to face all that these coming weeks will hold."*
- *"I want to slow down. I feel as if I'm on a speeding treadmill, and if I try to jump off I will stumble and fall."*
- *"I need help with my frazzled, frenzied state."*
- *"My busyness has robbed me of my joy."*

Why do we live such hectic, harried lives? Is this what God intended for us?

These kinds of responses are not unusual among the women I talk with. I could have written some of them myself—one or more of them may describe the way you're feeling today. So, why do we live such hectic, harried lives? Is this what God intended for us? And is there a way to get off that speeding treadmill without hurting ourselves (and others) in the process?

BUSY DAYS

The first chapter of the Gospel of Mark gives us a glimpse into a day in the life of the Lord Jesus. In some respects, this day was not unlike many of the days that you and I experience.

We pick up the account in verse 21:

> They went into Capernaum, and right away he entered the synagogue on the Sabbath and began to teach. [The people] were astonished at his teaching because he was teaching them as one who had authority, and not like the scribes. (Mark 1:21–22 CSB)

If you've ever taught a Bible study or a Sunday school class or led a small group, you know there's a lot more behind these words than what appears on the surface.

You know that you don't just get up before a group and teach the Word of God with power and effectiveness without time spent in preparation—not just preparation of the notes and the material, but preparation of your heart and life.

I love teaching the Scripture; to me there is nothing quite like seeing the Word of God penetrate and transform lives. But the process of preparing to speak is an intense one for me. I labor to determine what the Lord wants me to teach. I wrestle with the passages involved, seeking to understand what the Scripture means and to organize the material in a way that will be understandable and meaningful to the listener.

Then, while I'm actually teaching, I expend still more energy—physically, mentally, emotionally, and spiritually. And when I've finished speaking, the battle is still not over—that's often when the enemy seeks to discourage me with feelings of inadequacy or to tempt me with seeking the praise of others for my efforts. By the time it's all over, I'm often depleted and in need of restoration.

So, when I read that Jesus began this particular day by teaching in the synagogue, I know this was not just a nonchalant effort on His part. The people listened attentively to Him because they could tell this was not your normal, run-of-the-mill Sabbath message. Unlike the teachers they were accustomed to hearing, Jesus spoke with authority and power. We know that in order for this to be possible, He had spent concentrated time with His heavenly Father in preparation. As He ministered, He was being expended on behalf of others.

The apostle Paul later wrote, "I will most gladly spend and be spent for your souls" (2 Cor. 12:15). That's part of what is involved in ministering to others, whether in a synagogue in his day, or in our case, a small group study, a discipling setting, or a house full of little ones.

CONFRONTING EVIL

Speaking in the synagogue was just the beginning of Jesus' day, though. His work was not nearly over. Before He even had a chance to finish His message, there was an interruption in the service. Let's continue reading in Mark 1:

> Just then a man with an unclean spirit was in their synagogue. He cried out, "What do you have to do with us, Jesus of Nazareth? Have you come to destroy us? I know who you are—the Holy One of God!"
>
> Jesus rebuked him saying, "Be silent, and come out of him!" And the unclean spirit threw [the man] into convulsions, shouted with a loud voice, and came out of him.

> [The people] were all amazed, and so they began to ask each other: "What is this? A new teaching with authority! He commands even the unclean spirits, and they obey him." (Mark 1:23–27 CSB)

Here we see Jesus engaged in a battle between heaven and hell. This happened often during His years of earthly ministry because He lived and spoke and ministered in the power and the authority of God, which tended to stir the demons up. And this particular encounter with the enemy was not a casual, relaxed one. This was all-out warfare.

Now, I've never had an audible or visible encounter with a demon. Chances are, you haven't either. But that doesn't mean we are immune from spiritual battles. God's Word teaches that at this very moment there is cosmic warfare being waged between heaven and hell, that we are in the midst of a battle against "principalities and powers" (Eph. 3:10 NKJV) and sometimes God sends us right into the front lines of that battle. In the middle of our everyday lives, we sometimes find ourselves in difficult, demanding situations where we have to be alert to the schemes of Satan and skilled in using the sword of the Spirit to ward off his attacks.

There's a natural drain that is a part of being God's servant in these situations. And Jesus certainly experienced such a drain after His moments of confrontation with the powers of darkness.

Scripture tells us that as a result of this encounter with the demonized man, "at once the news about [Jesus] spread throughout the entire vicinity of Galilee" (v. 28). Imagine how that must have complicated Jesus' life. All of a sudden, people all over the area wanted Him to come speak at their synagogues and banquets, wanted to interview Him for their publications, wanted Him to heal their sick and cast out their demons. They all wanted a piece of Him. Later in this passage we learn that the time finally came when Jesus couldn't even stay in the cities. He had to seek out quiet, remote places in the countryside, where the crowds couldn't find Him, to get time alone with His Father.

Perhaps you've had the experience of ministering to someone in need—lending a listening ear to a discouraged young mother, helping out in your child's classroom, preparing a meal for a family in a crisis, being a youth sponsor on a mission trip, ministering to a friend's troubled teenager, or offering biblical counsel to a woman in a shaky marriage. The word spread that you were available to help people in need—and all of a sudden, your phone was lit up with texts from people wanting your time and help. If that's ever happened to you, then you may have an inkling of what Jesus felt as hurting people clamored for his time and attention.

EVERYBODY NEEDS ME!

Once the service at the synagogue was finally over, Jesus left the place and hurried "into Simon and Andrew's house with James and John" (Mark 1:29 CSB).

Whew! Jesus had spent hours giving out and expending Himself for others. Finally He has a chance to get away with His friends, away from all the needy people. Now he could go home, kick up His feet, and relax—maybe even take a nap. Right?

Wrong!

Read on: "Simon's mother-in-law was lying in bed with a fever, and they told [Jesus] about her at once" (v. 30 CSB).

Jesus was finally out of the public eye, back in the safe haven of a friend's home, and even there, someone needed Him.

No doubt you feel on occasion that there is no time, no place where you can totally escape the demands of other people. If it's not the people at work, it's your husband; if it's not your husband, it's your children; if it's not your children, it's the neighbor's children; if it's not someone else's children, it's your mother-in-law; if it's not your mother-in-law, it's . . .

But as we would expect, the serving heart of Jesus came out, and He made Himself available to meet the need. He took her hand, helped her up. "The fever left her, and she began to serve them" (v. 31 CSB).

With that, Jesus could finally settle in for a nice quiet evening alone with his friends. But then came the knocking at the door . . .

> When evening came, after the sun had set, [the people] brought to him all those who were sick and demon-possessed. The whole town was assembled at the door. (Mark 1:32–33 CSB)

I don't know how many people came to see Jesus that evening, but it sounds like a lot! Remember, this was still the same day. He had started early that morning—teaching, casting out demons, and healing the sick—and now it seems the whole city was lined up at His door wanting help.

Do you ever feel like the whole town is gathered at your door? Maybe it's your bathroom door, and you're just trying to get three minutes alone without having to answer any questions—but somebody's knocking on the door, the doorbell is ringing, notifications are popping up on your phone, the oven timer is buzzing, your three children seem like thirty-three, you feel like half the world is sick, and everybody needs you—all at the same time. You panic: "There's just not enough of me to go around!"

And yet Jesus didn't panic when He saw the needy outside the door. Instead, He

> healed many who were sick with various diseases and drove out many demons. (Mark 1:34 CSB)

HOW DID HE DO IT?

How did He do it? How did He stay sane? How did He keep His sense of equilibrium? How did He keep meeting the needs of so many people without falling apart Himself?

Yes, Jesus was God. But He was also human, which means He got tired; He got hungry; He felt the pressure of crowds constantly pressing around Him and having His privacy invaded. But He kept right on letting the crowds into His life. He kept on teaching, healing, confronting the powers of hell—and never a cross or impatient word. How did He do it?

Plus, Jesus was only given three years on this earth to accomplish the whole eternal plan of redemption. Talk about a long to-do list! Yet He never seemed hurried, harried, or overwhelmed with all there was to do in a day. Why not? How did He handle all the stress, strain, and responsibility without losing it?

I believe verse 35 gives us the key—not only to Jesus' life, but also to your life and mine, whatever our specific responsibilities and circumstances may be. That verse begins, "Very early in the morning . . ." (CSB).

I don't know about you, but when I've had a long, draining day, I know exactly what I want to do very early the next morning. *Nothing—except sleep!* Now, let me be clear: there's nothing wrong with sleeping when our bodies need it.

But Jesus knew there was something He needed that next morning even more than an extra hour of sleep. He had poured Himself out for countless needy individuals, and His spirit needed to be replenished. He knew it would never happen once the crowd woke up. So what did He do?

> Very early in the morning, while it was still dark, *he got up* ... (CSB)

He got up! The Scripture says that Jesus was tempted "in every respect" as we are (Heb. 4:15), so I have no doubt that He was tempted to sleep in. But He made a choice to say no to His body and yes to His Father. He got up. Then He "went out, and made his way to a deserted place; and there he was praying" (v. 35 CSB).

And it was none too soon. For it wasn't long before "Simon and his companions searched for him, and when they found him they said, 'Everyone is looking for you!'" (vv. 36–37 CSB). Yet, having just been in touch with His heavenly Father, Jesus knew exactly how He was to respond to the demands of the new day. He said,

> "Let's go on to the neighboring villages so that I may preach there too. This is why I have come." (v. 38 CSB)

Why were such morning appointments with His Father so crucial to Jesus' earthly ministry? Jesus knew that any power or ability He had to minister to others came from being one with the Father (John 10:30). He knew it was essential for Him to stay connected to His Source of life, joy, power, peace, and fruitfulness. He knew He had to walk in union and communion with His Father if He was to know and do His Father's will, which was His sole purpose for being on this earth. Nothing mattered more to Him than to live in intimate fellowship with His Father, so that He might fulfill what He had been sent to do.

For Jesus, time alone with God was essential. It was not something He tacked on to an overcrowded schedule. It was His lifeline to the Father, the highest priority of His life—more important than being with His disciples, more important than preaching the gospel, more important than time with His mother and brothers, more important than responding to the demands and needs of the crowds, more important than anything else.

The Gospel of Luke tells us that Jesus "would withdraw to desolate places and pray" (Luke 5:16). This was the pattern of His life. This is where He got His marching orders for each day, where He discovered the will of God for His life, where He got renewed and restored when "power went out from him" (Luke 6:19) as He ministered to the crowds. This is where He gained the resources to do battle against Satan—and win! It's where He stepped back from the corruption, clutter, and clamor of life on this earth and was given the ability to see the world from God's point of view. It's where He received grace to love the unlovable and power to do the impossible.

And this is precisely where you and I so often miss out on all that God has for us. We attempt to live life in our own energy. We think we can keep giving out without getting replenished. Then, wearied and weakened by the demands of life and ministry, we become impatient and annoyed with the very ones God has sent us to serve. Rather than exhibiting a gracious, calm, joyous spirit, we become uptight, frazzled, and frenzied, resenting rather than welcoming the people and opportunities God brings into our lives. I know. I've been there again and again.

Is it really possible for us to manifest the same spirit Jesus did when facing pressure? That all depends on whether we are willing to make the same choice He made, to adopt His number one priority as the number one priority of our lives:

> Very early in the morning, while it was still dark, he got up, went out, and made his way to a deserted place; and there he was praying. (Mark 1:35 CSB)

MAKE IT PERSONAL

1. Which of the following best describes the condition of your personal devotional life these days?

   - For all practical purposes, I have no devotional life.
   - My devotional life is inconsistent and sporadic.
   - I'm spending time in the Word and prayer on a consistent basis, but I often feel that I'm just going through the motions. My devotions are more a matter of duty than delight.

- I'm meeting alone with the Lord on a daily basis and am cultivating a meaningful, intimate relationship with Him through His Word, prayer, and praise.

2. What are three or four words that would typically describe your spirit when your schedule is full or you're in the midst of pressured circumstances (for example: calm, prayerful, frenzied, demanding)?

3. Based on the account we've just read in Mark 1, how would you describe the way Jesus responded to pressure?

4. What do you think accounted for His ability to respond to interruptions, demands, and the incessant needs of those around Him?

5. Take a few moments to pray and ask God to speak to you through this study. Ask Him to make you like Jesus in your response to the circumstances of life and to give you a deeper desire to make your relationship with Him the most important priority of your life.

CHAPTER 2

Made for Intimacy

Everyone loves a love story. Love stories are the stuff that movies and bestsellers and headlines are made of. That's because we were made to give and receive love. We were made for intimacy.

Yet most of us know more about the absence of intimacy than the reality. That sense of aloneness and isolation we have all experienced somewhere in the core of our being is a God-created hole that cries out to be filled; it is a longing for intimacy. We crave closeness, warmth, and affection. We long to know that we matter to someone, that someone cares, that someone who really knows us still loves us.

But early on in life we begin to learn that other humans can never completely fulfill those longings—not even in the best of families or the closest of relationships.

That's because the God who created that hole in our hearts is also the only One who can fill it.

In the Scriptures we encounter a God who moves toward us, who seeks to draw us to Himself, who knows us intimately, and who invites us to know Him. We are introduced to Him in the first pages of the book of Genesis, where He initiates relationship with the first man and the first woman. Of all God's creation, humans alone are given the capacity to respond to God's initiative, to love Him in return, to know Him, and to enjoy His companionship.

However, no sooner has the story begun than the humans reject God's initiative, and intimacy is broken. In response, this Lover-God immediately sets into motion a plan that He devised in eternity past—a means by which His estranged loved ones may be restored to fellowship with Himself.

And what is the outcome of that plan—its ultimate fulfillment? We see it in the final pages of Revelation, which depicts heaven being peopled with those whose hearts have been won by God's love and who will spend eternity in an untarnished relationship with their Creator.

You see, from start to finish, the Word of God is one incredible love story. And, wonder of wonders, it is a story that has your name and mine in it. Whether you grew up in the church or have no church background at all, whether you are well versed in the Bible or have only recently opened it for the first time, there is room in this love story for you.

So many stories of Scripture illustrate what it is to be loved by God and to respond to His divine initiative with wonder, worship, and glad surrender. They show us men and women who drank from the deep wells of that divine love, who longed to linger in His presence and counted it their highest privilege and aim to live in unbroken union and communion with Him. Their lives make us thirsty for intimacy with the Creator-Lover who corresponds to that hole in our hearts.

ADAM AND EVE: ALONE WITH THEIR CREATOR

Adam and Eve were the first of God's creatures to experience this remarkable union. Nowhere do we read of God's conversing with the trees, the fish, or the oceans. Nowhere do we see God seeking out a relationship with any of His creation except for the man and the woman, created in His own image.

Only to Adam and Eve did God reveal Himself, His character, His wishes, His ways. There was no fear between God and the couple, only perfect love. There was no guilt, no shame, for the man and his wife delighted to know and to do the will of God and basked in His approval. They welcomed the presence and the voice of God. Communion with Him was the reason for their existence.

Perhaps you have experienced something of that kind of relationship with God. You have been the recipient of His incredible love and blessing. You know what it is to walk with Him, to listen to His Word, and to respond with the worship of a satisfied heart.

Do you also know what it is to lose that intimacy? Do you know what it is to make a choice that creates distance where there was once nearness, fear where there was once trust, and shame where there was once freedom?

That moment when the first man and first woman signed their own emancipation proclamation was a decisive one. They chose to believe the word of the serpent rather than the word of God. They acted apart from their Creator-Lover and became separated from Him. And when they heard the sound of God walking in the garden in the early morning hours, they were fearful and could not bear to face Him or each other. Instead, they covered their naked bodies and attempted to hide from God.

As descendants of those first parents, we have all experienced that fearful, dreadful sense of shame that makes us want to hide from God because we know we have spurned the only true love we have ever known. In that dark instant, we may feel that we have thrown His love away and will never experience it again.

But even in that moment of shameful separation in the garden, there was hope, as God the eternal Lover took the initiative to restore the estranged couple to fellowship. He tenderly, lovingly clothed them in the skins of animals (requiring that blood be shed) and set in motion the means whereby humankind might ultimately be reunited with Him. And even as they faced the painful consequences of their choices, God never stopped loving, never stopped communicating, never stopped seeking, never stopped initiating. Just as He never stops loving and seeking you and me.

ABRAHAM: FRIEND OF GOD

Centuries later, in keeping with His great, eternal plan, God revealed Himself to another person. I have often tried to imagine what Abraham must have felt the very first time he heard the voice of God. He was not looking for God. He did even know God. He had been reared in a pagan, idolatrous culture where no one knew God. There were no believers, no Bibles, no hymnals, no churches, no preachers.

Then one day God pierced the silence. He introduced Himself to Abraham and made some incredible promises. And Abraham listened. When no one else was paying attention, when no one else believed, Abraham was given grace to respond to God's initiative. The story of his life is the story of a man who hearkened to the voice of God as He revealed His secrets, His plans, and His will. It is the story of a man who responded to that voice with worship, faith, love, and obedience. Altars erected at Shechem, Bethel, Hebron, and Mount Moriah trace the steps of this "friend of God" (James 2:23)—a man who walked with God in intimate communion and fellowship.

It's not that Abraham never wavered in his faith. On more than one occasion, in fact, he acted as if he didn't know God at all. But God's love was not based on Abraham's performance. Even when Abraham started acting like a pagan, God still pursued him passionately and relentlessly.

Just as He pursued Adam and Eve.

Just as He pursues you and me.

DAVID: "ONE THING HAVE I DESIRED"

Fourteen generations after Abraham, another friend of God continued a line that would lead to the Lord Jesus Himself. As a military strategist and warrior, as a musician and poet, and as a statesman and king—in virtually every way—David stood head and shoulders above his peers. This man had it all—fame, popularity, fortune, natural ability, and loyal friends. Yet in one of his famous songs he wrote,

> One thing I have desired of the LORD,
> That will I seek. (Ps. 27:4 NKJV)

What was that one thing? What was the deepest desire and longing of this outstanding man's heart? What mattered more than anything else to a man who seemingly had everything? What was his highest earthly priority? If only one thing could be said of him at the end of his life, what would he want it to be?

By the way, how would *you* finish that sentence? "One thing have I asked of the Lord, that will I seek after: _____." What is the greatest desire and longing of your heart? In our answer to that question lies the explanation for much of what we do—our choices, our priorities, our use of time, the way we spend money, the way we respond to pressure, whom or what we love.

David's answer reveals why God called David a man after His own heart (1 Sam. 13:14; Acts 13:22). The one thing he desired was

> That I may dwell in the house of the Lord
> All the days of my life,
> To behold the beauty of the Lord,
> And to enquire in His temple. (Ps. 27:4 NKJV)

In spite of all he possessed, all he had done, all the people he had known, all the places he had been, and all the privileges and opportunities he had enjoyed, David had one supreme, driving passion in life: to walk in union and communion with God. In other words: "If I can only accomplish one thing in my life, if nothing else gets done, this is the one thing that really matters to me. My highest goal and my number one priority is to *live* in the Lord's presence, to *look* on His beauty and to *learn* from Him. I want to know Him, to love Him, to have an intimate relationship with Him. That's the one thing in my life that matters most. And that is the one thing I am going to pursue above all others."

Like Abraham, David had his flaws. He blew it in some of the most crucial relationships of life. But God would not let him go. With a confronting, convicting, consuming, cleansing love, God kept pursuing David, even when the man's actions might cause us to wonder, Why bother with *him*? The answer is the same reason He bothers with us—because He is a Lover in pursuit of relationship—a God who never stops loving and pursuing.

MARY AND MARTHA OF BETHANY: "ONLY ONE THING IS NEEDED"

The New Testament introduces us to another familiar figure, this time a woman who enjoyed a beautiful relationship with her Lord and who treasured time spent alone in His presence. Actually, the story of Mary of Bethany is closely intertwined with that of her sister, Martha. It is a story that speaks to me in a fresh way each time I read it.

We first meet the two women in Luke 10:38–42, where we are told that "Martha opened her home to [Jesus]" (v. 38). What a lovely thing to be said of any follower of Christ. Martha—the sister with an extraordinary flair for hospitality.

How we need women like her in every generation who are willing to open their hearts and homes to the Lord and others. Sadly, though, when so many of us are chronically overwhelmed by competing demands of family, work, and more, there are precious few who have a heart, the time, or the practical skills to practice hospitality—serving and caring for others, whether in their home, at church, in a restaurant, or in a park.

However, as needed and valuable as is the ministry of

hospitality, Martha's story reminds us that a hospitable bent can also have its pitfalls.

As the passage unfolds, we see a dramatic scene that I recognize all too well. A band of hungry men descended on Martha's home. I can just imagine this highly organized, efficient woman as she flew into action, giving direction to everyone within earshot: "There's no time to waste—no time to dawdle. The bread must be kneaded and baked, the meat prepared and grilled, the vegetables scrubbed and roasted . . . the floors cleaned, tables set, drinks poured . . ."

As we read the passage, we can sense that on this particular day things just weren't falling together quite right. There was no way everything would be ready on time. And Martha was becoming edgy and agitated—"distracted with much serving" (v. 40)—or, as the King James Version puts it, "Martha was *cumbered* about much serving." That word *cumbered* literally means "to be pulled apart."[1]

Do you know that feeling? I certainly do. We start out with the best intentions to serve those around us. But one circumstance piles on top of another until we become so consumed with the mechanics and details of our work that we begin to feel pulled apart and lose sight of why we were serving in the first place.

I've had it happen in the kitchen, in the midst of preparing refreshments for a Bible study group. I've had it happen in my study while preparing messages for an upcoming conference or podcast. I've had it happen in a meeting with ministry colleagues, planning for a major ministry event.

Perhaps it was when the stew boiled over or the bread burned that Martha's simmering frustration finally began to boil. And that was when she looked around and realized that her younger sister was nowhere to be seen.

"Where's Mary?" she demanded of the nearest servant.

"She's in the living room with the men."

That did it. Martha had had it with her less driven sibling! She hurried into the living room to give Mary a piece of her mind. But when the explosion came, it was directed not at Mary, but at Jesus. "Lord," she complained, "do you not care that my sister has left me to serve alone?" (v. 40).

When we become preoccupied with earthly things rather than eternal matters, we easily become resentful, self-centered, and angry. Our party turns into a pity party, and we start to believe that no one—not even Jesus—knows or cares about all the sacrifices we've made. That's exactly what was happening with Martha. "Tell her then to help me!" she demanded of Jesus. (Have you ever found yourself telling God what to do?)

> When we become preoccupied with earthly things rather than eternal matters, we easily become resentful, self-centered, and angry.

The reason most of us relate to the story thus far is that we know what it is to have our inner spirit in turmoil—to become irritated, angry, and demanding; to feel as if our circumstances and emotions have spun out of control. Then, after the explosion, we may feel terrible and think, "What got into me? Why did I act that way? Why did I get so uptight and frustrated over burnt rolls?"

Jesus' words to Martha speak to all of us. Patiently He addressed her: "Martha, Martha, you are anxious and troubled about many things [*It's true, I* am *anxious and troubled about many things*], but *one thing* is necessary [*Just one thing?*]. Mary has chosen the good portion, which will not be taken away from her" (Luke 10:41–42).

What is it that Mary had chosen? What had Mary been doing all this time? She was simply sitting at the feet of Jesus, listening to what he said (v. 39).

It's as if Jesus were saying, "Martha, My friend, there are *so many things* on your mind, so many tasks on your to-do list. Listen, there's nothing wrong with your wanting to serve us dinner. The problem, Martha, is that you've allowed your list to pull you apart and to distract you from the *one thing* in this world that matters most—knowing Me, listening to Me, having a relationship with Me. That's the *only thing* that is absolutely essential. If you don't get anything else done on your list, don't miss that one thing!"

Jesus reminded Martha that Mary had *chosen* to cultivate her relationship with Him, even when other things might have distracted her focus. Developing intimacy with the Lord requires a conscious, deliberate choice. It's a choice to spend time sitting at His feet and listening to His Word, even when there are other good things vying for our attention. It's a choice to put Him first, above anything and everything else in our busy lives.

I can almost hear Jesus saying to Martha, "We don't have to have a five-course meal tonight. It's okay if dinner's late, if the kitchen's a mess, or even if we don't have dinner at all. What matters is My relationship with you. That's why I came to your house. That's why I came to this world. Your company means more to Me than your cooking. You're more important to Me than anything you can do for Me."

And so we're right back where we started, realizing that God is a Lover who created us for relationship with Himself. That's what the Christian life is about. It is not about all the things we do for God. It's about being loved and redeemed by Him, loving Him in return, and walking in intimate union and communion with Him.

Mary's choice was not made out of obligation, but out of devotion. She was not sitting at Jesus' feet out of a sense of duty, but because she cherished her relationship with Him.

Shortly before Jesus went to the cross, Mary attended another dinner where He was a guest, this time at the home of Simon the leper (John 12:1–8). Once again we find Martha serving (though I'd like to think she served this meal with a different heart). And once again we find Mary at the feet of Jesus, this time anointing His feet with a pound of costly ointment. That act, though it incurred the indignation of some who watched, was precious to Jesus, for He knew His love had captured and kept her heart.

DEVOTIONS WITHOUT DEVOTION

Some of us have had *devotions,* but we've not had *devotion.* There's a big difference. We may have gone through the motions of reading our Bibles and "saying our prayers," but we've not been cultivating a relationship with our Lover-God. We know a lot *about* Him, but we don't really know *Him.* We're active and busy in a multitude of "spiritual" activities, but we've lost perspective of who it is that we're serving and why.

The result of our "devotionless" religion is often seen in the way we respond to pressure. So many of us Christian women are perpetually stressed out. I see it in the eyes of women everywhere, I hear it in their voices, and too often I see it when I look in the mirror. I know what it is to have demands coming at me from every direction. I know what it is to respond out of weariness, with an impatient, demanding spirit. And I know what it is to contend with God Himself, even as my eyes well up with tears of frustration with those around me and with myself and my reactions.

I also know that there's only one place where that angry, reactive, overwhelmed self can be transformed—the same place that Mary chose, at the feet of Jesus. I must make a conscious, deliberate, daily choice to sit at His feet, to listen to His Word, to receive His love, to let Him change me, and to pour out my heart's devotion to Him.

When I get into His presence, the whole world looks different. When I draw close to His heart, I find mercy when I know I deserve judgment. I find forgiveness for all my petty, selfish ways; I find grace for my inadequacies; I find peace for my troubled heart and perspective for my distorted views. In Him I find an eye in the midst of the storm. Oh, the storm around me may not immediately subside; but the storm *within* me is calmed.

> When I draw close to His heart, I find mercy when I know I deserve judgment. I find forgiveness for all my petty, selfish ways; I find grace for my inadequacies; I find peace for my troubled heart and perspective for my distorted views.

AN INVITATION TO INTIMACY

And so the Father-Lover heart of God continues to call us into relationship with Himself. He is seeking lovers. He desires our company; He longs to hear our voice and see our face.

Not until we make pursuing Him our highest priority and goal in life will we begin to fulfill the purpose for which He created us. Nothing—absolutely nothing—is more important. And that relationship for which we were created cannot be cultivated or sustained apart from spending consistent time alone with Him.

Where are you in your relationship with God? Is it warm, vibrant, and growing, or has it become distant and passionless? Are you nurturing that relationship by spending time each day alone with Him? Is He giving you a new desire to know Him and His love and to offer true devotion to Him? If so, why not take David's mission statement (Ps.27:4) and make it your prayer:

> Lord Jesus, You have shown me that only one thing is absolutely necessary, and that is the one thing I want to seek after with all my heart: that I may live in Your presence every day of my life, that I may gaze upon Your beauty with a heart of worship and adoration, and that I may learn to know Your heart, Your ways, and Your will. By Your grace may this be the highest daily priority of my life. Amen.

MAKE IT PERSONAL

1. Think of someone you know who seems to have a close, personal relationship with the Lord. To what do you attribute his or her nearness to God?

2. Martha was "pulled apart" by all her meal preparations. What are some of the things that pull you apart and keep you from sitting at the feet of Jesus and listening to Him?

3. If those closest to you were to look at the way you spend your time, what would they say are the most important priorities in your life?

4. Describe a time in your life when taking time out to "sit at the feet of Jesus" made a noticeable difference in your perspective or your ability to respond to your circumstances.

PART TWO

The Purpose of a Devotional Life

*Show me now your ways,
that I may know you.*
EX. 33:13

The young believer must understand that he has no power of his own to maintain his spiritual life. No, he needs each day to receive new grace from heaven through fellowship with the Lord Jesus. This cannot be obtained by a hasty prayer, or a superficial reading of a few verses from God's Word. He must take time quietly and deliberately to come into God's presence, to feel his weakness and his need, and to wait upon God through His Holy Spirit, to renew the heavenly light and life in his heart. Then he may rightly expect to be kept by the power of Christ throughout all the day, and all its temptations.

ANDREW MURRAY

CHAPTER 3

The Inner Life

Deep down, have you ever had any of these thoughts?

- If I have my devotions, God will be pleased with me. If I don't have my devotions, God will be disappointed with me.
- Having a daily quiet time makes me more spiritual. If I don't have this time, I'll be less spiritual.
- If I have my quiet time today, God will help me out and my day will go better. If I don't have devotions, God won't help me, and I'm sure to have all sorts of problems.
- I have to have daily devotions—every good Christian does.

We've looked at the *priority* of spending time alone with God on a consistent basis. We've seen that Jesus maintained regular times of communication with His Father. We've observed that knowing God was what mattered most to godly men and women in the Scripture. And we've said that spending time with God must be the number one priority of our lives if we are to fulfill our God-created purpose.

Now let's look more specifically at the *purpose* of spending time alone with God. I've found that one of the reasons many people experience a sense of frustration and failure in relation to their devotional life is that they don't understand *why* this practice is so important. As a result, there are sincere believers who set out to have daily devotions for all the wrong reasons.

Thoughts such as those listed above put many believers in bondage and keep them from entering into the real purpose for setting aside time each day to meet with God.

We need to understand that the purpose of daily devotions is *not* to gain points with God, nor is it a way to keep God from disapproving of us. It's not a way of earning His favor or getting Him to love us more. If we belong to Him, we already *have* His favor; He could not love us any more than He does, and He could not love us any less.

Further, setting aside time for personal devotions doesn't necessarily make us any more spiritual. (The Pharisees were renowned for their "spiritual disciplines," but they were far from godly.) Neither is a quiet time some sort of good-luck charm that gets God on our side, guarantees our day will go better, and keeps us from having problems. Daily devotions are not a way of bartering or negotiating with God.

> The purpose of daily devotions is not to earn His favor or get Him to love us more. If we belong to Him, we already have His favor; He could not love us any more than He does, and He could not love us any less.

Then what *is* the purpose of a devotional practice? What makes it worth making the effort to get up earlier in the morning, to find time in an already packed schedule, and to prioritize a daily quiet time? What can we hope to see accomplished through that time? And why is this habit such a crucial one in the life of a believer?

I'd like to suggest eight purposes. The first four, which we'll unpack in this chapter, relate primarily to our inner life with God. In the next chapter we'll take a look at four additional purposes that not only affect our inner life, but also flow out into our lifestyle and our relationships with others.

COMMUNION

The most important purpose of a daily devotional life is not to check another task off our to-do list, but rather to experience intimate union and communion with God. Remember, we are talking about a relationship. The God of the universe *loves you*, and He desires friendship with you.

"Is that really possible?" you might ask. "How can someone like me have a close friendship with Him?" Moses must have wondered the same thing.

Over the course of his lifetime, this rescuer-leader-lawgiver-prophet experienced an extraordinary closeness with God. But their relationship didn't start out that way. In fact, Moses' first encounter with God could hardly be called intimate. As he stood next to that piece of burning brush on the side of a mountain and heard the voice of God, Moses was terrified. He "hid his face, for he was afraid to look at God" (Ex. 3:6).

But once God had Moses' attention, He began to share things no other man of his time had ever known. He revealed His compassionate heart and His deep concern about the sufferings of the children of Israel in Egypt. He disclosed His desire to deliver His people from slavery and His plan to use Moses as His instrument. And He made clear that He had all the power and resources to make it happen.

As Moses considered his checkered past and his self-perceived deficiencies, he must have wondered how this could be. He felt insecure, overwhelmed, and inadequate. (Ever had those feelings yourself?) Nonetheless, he responded to God's initiative, and from that day his life was never the same—just as your life will never be the same once you embark on the adventure of a growing, vital relationship with God.

For the most part, over the next forty years Moses communed alone with God. With the exception of his understudy, Joshua, there were few others who had the same heart to know Yahweh. Perhaps you know what it is to walk alone with God, without the fellowship of a godly mate, children, or close friends. If so, let Moses' story be an encouragement to you. You can still enjoy personal communion with God, even if those around you don't share your desire for a close relationship with Him.

After leading the children of Israel out of Egypt and across the Red Sea, Moses continued to devote himself to pursuing communion with God. At times that meant responding to God's call to spend weeks alone with Him in remote mountain settings.

During one of those protracted times, God gave Moses directions for constructing a tabernacle. God described the purpose of this tent structure: "There I will meet with you, to speak to you.... There I will meet with the people of Israel" (Ex. 29:42–43). The whole point of the tabernacle (and later of the temple) was that there might be a place on this earth set aside for communion between God and His people. For centuries after that, if an Israelite wanted to meet with God, to fellowship with Him, he would go to the place God had established for that purpose.

When we come to the New Testament, we learn that we no longer need to go to a physical tent or place of meeting to commune with God. Because Christ has come and shed His blood for our sins, the way has been opened up for us to approach the Father directly. By His indwelling Holy Spirit, you and I have become the temple of God, the place where God lives.

The purpose of this new temple is the same as it was with the temple of old—to be a place where we can meet with God. This is the heart of Jesus' words to the church in Laodicea: "Behold, I stand at the door and knock. If anyone hears my voice and opens the door, I will come in to him and eat with him, and he with me" (Rev. 3:20). Eating a meal together is a universal symbol of friendship and fellowship. As with Moses, the purpose of our quiet time is not to jump through spiritual hoops or to fulfill some sort of heavenly homework assignment, but to sit down and eat a fellowship meal with the Lord—to commune with Him.

As a result of extended time spent in the presence of God, Moses enjoyed an unusually deep friendship with God. Whereas others in the camp could not draw near to God or look on His glory, "the LORD used to speak to Moses face to face, as a man speaks with his friend" (Ex. 33:11). Moses was not allowed to see God's face (vv. 21–33), but God spoke with Moses directly, not through an intermediary.

Face-to-Face Friendship

"Face to face" in Exodus 33:11 is a picture of intimacy. It's a picture of lovers. On the other hand, when something comes between two friends, it can be awkward and uncomfortable to be face-to-face. I remember hearing a wife describe a conflict she had had with her husband the night before. She said, "I lay down on our bed and turned my face toward the wall and my back toward my husband!" It doesn't take a therapist to know there was a problem in that relationship. The intimacy has been breached.

You've seen the same principle at work in children. When your child does something wrong, where's the last place in the world he wants to look? Into your eyes. Holding his little face in your hands, you say firmly, "Look into Mommy's eyes!" But he avoids looking into your face. Why? Because something has come between the two of you, and the fellowship has been broken.

If you've walked with God for any length of time, you know what it is to have a breach in the relationship—to find it difficult to look Him "in the eye." The purpose of a daily devotional time is to turn back toward Him, to address whatever has caused the breach, and to reestablish fellowship. Then we can once again look into His face without shame or fear.

We see in Moses a man who was always yearning for a deeper fellowship with God. In one of his most intimate recorded conversations with Yahweh, Moses pleaded, "If I have found favor in your sight, please show me now your ways, that I may know you" (Ex. 33:13). This is the prayer of a man who didn't just want to know more *about* God. He wanted to *know* God.

As you meet with God in your daily devotional time, don't forget that the ultimate purpose is not simply to gain more knowledge about God or His Word, but to know *Him* and to enjoy intimate communion with Him. You may be a seasoned student of the Word. You may even be a Bible study leader. But if your study of the Word does not lead you to *know God*, you've missed the whole purpose.

In the front of my Bible, I've written a hymn fragment that expresses my longing to know God through His Word:

> Beyond the sacred page
> I seek *Thee*, Lord;
> My spirit pants for *Thee*,
> O living Word.[1]

PURIFICATION

Do you sometimes feel like all you ever do is clean? That's because things (and people) tend to get dirty. Whether we're speaking of clothes, children's hands, kitchen floors, bathrooms, vinyl siding, entryways, or our own bodies, dealing with the dust, crumbs, and grime that accumulate is a necessary and never-ending process.

That's true of *us* as well. The second purpose of a devotional life is purification, the cleansing of our hearts and our lives.

Now, as far as our *position* before God is concerned, we've already been declared clean—Jesus Christ has taken all our unrighteousness upon Himself and clothed us in His righteousness.

As far as our future *prospect* is concerned, our purity is also assured. After all, God chose us "before the foundation of the world" and determined "that we should be holy and blameless before him" (Eph. 1:4). He predestined us to be a holy bride for His holy Son—pure and clean. And one day we will be just that.

However, as far as our *practice* is concerned, we don't always live up to our holy position and our holy prospect.

You and I live in a corrupt world. We inhabit a contaminated flesh. And we have a way of getting our spiritual feet, hands, and clothes dirty on a regular basis.

At the Last Supper, taking the role of a slave, Jesus went around the table and washed the feet of each of His disciples. When it was Peter's turn, the outspoken disciple wasn't comfortable with the whole idea of the Master washing his feet. Thus followed an important lesson about personal cleansing.

In response to Peter's protest, Jesus told him that apart from being washed, he could have no part with Christ. The pure, spotless, undefiled Son of God cannot walk in oneness with impure, defiled believers. "Can two walk together, unless they are agreed?" the prophet Amos asked (Amos 3:3 NKJV). And another prophet, Isaiah, explained to worshipers who wanted to know why God wasn't listening to their prayers,

> Your iniquities have made a separation between you and God. (Isa. 59:2)

When Peter realized the cost of refusing to be washed, he decided he wanted to go all the way. "Lord," he said, "not my feet only but also my hands and my head!" (John 13:9).

Jesus went on to explain that "the one who has bathed does not need to wash, except for his feet, but is completely clean. And you are clean" (v. 10). In other words, once we enter into a relationship with Christ through His shed blood, we have been eternally cleansed. But when we allow our lives to become soiled by this world or by our sinful choices, we need to return to be washed once more.

In the Old Testament tabernacle, we find a striking illustration of this process of washing. Before entering into the Holy Place to represent the people before God, the priest would first stop at the bronze altar where an innocent animal would be offered up as a sacrifice for the priest's own sin and for the sin of the people. Then he would move to a bronze basin known as a laver, where he would wash his hands. He would return to that laver as needed throughout the day.

That's a picture of what happens during our devotional time with the Lord. Although our sin has been atoned for by the blood of Jesus, when we come into His presence, He takes us to the "laver" so that we might wash our hands and feet of whatever may have defiled us.

Washed with the Water of the Word

What is the "water" God uses to purify us? It's the water of the Word. Jesus prayed for His disciples, "Sanctify them in the truth; your word is truth" (John 17:17). In His final discourse with the disciples before going to Gethsemane, Jesus said, "Already you are clean because of the word that I have spoken to you" (John 15:3).

The book of Ephesians teaches that "Christ loved the church and gave himself up for her" (Eph. 5:25). His death on the cross was birthed out of His commitment to a love relationship. The next verse goes on to reveal His ultimate purpose for the church and how He intends to fulfill that purpose: "That he might sanctify her, having cleansed her by the washing of water *with the word*" (v. 26). The Holy Spirit takes the Word and applies it to our hearts to cleanse and purify them.

As I spend time alone with God in the morning, I ask Him who sees and knows all to expose anything in my heart that is not holy. He knows me better than I know myself. My natural instinct would be to cover my sin, so I ask Him to shine the light of His holiness into my heart and to show me what He sees there, approaching Him with the attitude of the psalmist:

> Who can discern his errors?
>   Declare me innocent from hidden faults. (Ps. 19:12)
>
> Search me, O God, and know my heart!
>   Try me and know my thoughts!
> And see if there be any grievous way in me,
>   and lead me in the way everlasting. (Ps. 139:23–24)

Day after day, as I soak in His Word and open up my heart to the work of His Spirit, He is faithful to bring to my attention things that have grieved Him—a harsh word spoken to a colleague, a selfish choice or expenditure, a proud or unloving attitude toward another, a covetous heart, unbelief, an impatient response, seeking human praise or admiration, taking credit for what He has done, an ungrateful spirit, unforgiveness or resentment, demanding rights . . .

Having seen what the light reveals, I agree with God, confess it as sin, and ask Him to wash me by the blood and the Word of Christ. Where my sin has affected others, I purpose to seek their forgiveness. Then I am free to walk before Him, without guilt or shame, and with a pure heart and a conscience that is clear toward God and all people.

Having cleansed us from sin by the washing of His Word, God then uses the Scripture to protect our hearts from sinning against Him.

> How can a young man keep his way pure?
>   By guarding it according to your word. (Ps. 119:9)

RESTORATION

Ask most women how they're doing, and there's a good chance the answer will be along the lines of: "Whew! I've got so much going on!" or "I'm exhausted!" Overcrowded schedules and stressed-out lives seem to be the norm. As we walk through each day, responding to the needs of those around us, we can become physically, emotionally, and spiritually depleted.

I'm convinced that one of the major reasons we get overwhelmed by day-to-day demands is that our spirits are weary. Our souls need to be restored. And that's another purpose of setting aside time to be alone in God's presence each day. He has a never-ending supply of grace, strength, and wisdom available that He wants to flow through us to others. But we need to keep coming back into His presence to get our supply replenished.

The circumstances and demands of a typical day may cause us to fall wearily into bed at night. When we awake in the morning, His mercies are new and fresh (Lam. 3:23). But if we fail to stop and draw from His fresh, infinite supply of mercy and grace, we'll find ourselves having to operate out of our own meager resources.

David the psalmist knew what it was to get his soul restored in the presence of God. Many of his psalms begin with fear, anger, vexation, or confusion. But as he pours out his heart to the Lord, his whole perspective is changed, and he receives an infusion of supernatural hope and strength.

Listen to David's prayer when he's out in the wilderness fleeing from an insanely jealous king who's obsessed with taking his life:

> O God, you are my God; earnestly I seek you;
>   my soul thirsts for you;
> my flesh faints for you,
>   as in a dry and weary land where there is no water....
> Because your steadfast love is better than life,
>   my lips will praise you....
>   My soul will be satisfied as with fat and rich food....
> For you have been my help,
>   and in the shadow of your wings I will sing for joy.
>   (Ps. 63:1, 3, 5, 7)

You can sense the restoration taking place as he cries out to God in the midst of another crisis:

> Hear my cry, O God,
>   listen to my prayer;
> from the end of the earth I call to you
>   when my heart is faint.
> Lead me to the rock
>   that is higher than I,
> for you have been my refuge,
>   a strong tower against the enemy.
> Let me dwell in your tent forever!
>   Let me take refuge under the shelter of your
>   wings! (Ps. 61:1–4)

The restoration of our souls is a ministry of our great Shepherd, described so tenderly in Psalm 23:

> The LORD is my shepherd, I shall not want....
>   He restores my soul. (vv. 1, 3)

The Hebrew word translated "restore" in verse 3 is a word that is more often rendered "return" in the Old Testament. It's used to speak of God's people returning to Him and of

God returning to His people. The word suggests "movement back to the point of departure."[2] The implication here is that God restores our souls back to their original resting place—in Him. He does so by means of His Spirit and His Word:

> He makes me lie down in green pastures.
> He leads me beside still waters (v. 2)

Notice that the sheep don't get fed, refreshed, and restored on the run. They have to slow down at times, to stop, be still, lie down.

Often I've found myself giving out and giving out and giving out, but not taking time to get back to the still, quiet waters where my Shepherd wants to restore my soul. If I don't do what it takes to get my spiritual tank refilled, I end up running on fumes. Before long, the least little demand is more than I can handle, and I find myself reacting to even minor annoyances and interruptions out of frustration and irritation. But in that daily time alone with Him, He calms my spirit, slows down my racing pulse, and gives me fresh perspective and renewed desire and strength to serve Him for another day.

Even as you read these words, is your soul in need of restoration? Why not take a few minutes to reread the two prayers of David quoted above? Try reading them aloud. As you do, let your Great Shepherd restore your soul.

INSTRUCTION

Wouldn't it be great if you could sign up for a class that would teach you everything you need to know and provide answers for all your problems? Maybe you've got a boss who's impossible to please, a food addiction you just can't kick, a teen (or husband) who plays video games endlessly, a church where no one seems to be hungry for God, a child who has started lying, or bills that always seem larger than the paycheck.

The fact is, there *is* a "course" that addresses every issue we will ever face. The Teacher loves to meet one-on-one with His students, so He can tailor the study to our needs. He is willing to hold class every day that we are willing to meet. We already have the Textbook, which was written by the Teacher Himself. Parts of it can be difficult to grasp. But the Teacher is always available—twenty-four hours a day—to help us understand.

Establishing a daily devotional habit enrolls us in this course. During this time we sit at the feet of the Lord Jesus and ask Him to instruct us, to teach us what He is like and how to live in a way that pleases Him.

The Textbook—the Word of God—doesn't claim to solve all our problems. But it does offer all the resources we need to face those problems. And it will teach us something that is absolutely essential to dealing with the circumstances of life: *the ways of God.*

Psalm 103:7 tells us that God

> made known his *ways* to Moses,
> his *acts* to the people of Israel.

Note the distinction between Moses who knew the *ways* of God and others who simply knew His *acts*.

The Israelites saw God send the plagues on the Egyptians when Pharaoh hardened his heart against God. They saw Him part the waters of the Red Sea when there was no other way of escape from the Egyptian army. When they were hungry, they saw God provide manna for bread and quail for meat. When they were thirsty, they saw Him bring water gushing forth from a rock, When Miriam challenged Moses' right to lead, they saw God strike her with leprosy. They were well acquainted with the *acts* of God. But they knew little of the *ways* of God.

God revealed His ways to Moses because Moses had an attentive heart, a listening ear, and a passion to know Him. Moses was willing to pay the price to know God's ways. He was willing to spend much time alone with God, away from the crowd, patiently waiting for Him to speak.

"Show Me Your Ways"

One of the greatest desires of my heart is that I might know the ways of God. I want to know His thoughts, His feelings, His heart, and even His secrets. I want to know His perspective on this world; on history, on current affairs; on the future, on work, relaxation, relationships, my family, the church, and ministry—on everything. I want to know what brings Him joy and what causes Him to grieve. I want to know His ways. I don't believe God owes me an explanation about anything. But I do want to know everything about Him and His heart that He is willing to reveal.

That's why countless times over the years, before opening the Word of God, I've prayed the words of David in Psalm 25:

> Show me your ways, O Lord;
> Teach me your paths.
> Lead me in your truth and teach me. (vv. 4–5 NKJV)

That psalm goes on to tell us the kind of man or woman that God will teach:

> The humble He guides in justice,
> And the humble He teaches his way....
> Who is the man that fears the LORD?
> Him shall He teach in the way He chooses....
> The secret of the LORD is with those who fear him,
> And He will show him his covenant. (vv. 9, 12, 14 NKJV)

Whom does the Lord teach? He instructs those whose hearts are humble—those who have a teachable spirit, who know how little they know and how much they need to learn. And He teaches those who fear Him—those who reverence and stand in awe of Him. These are the ones He confides in and trusts with His secrets.

I've been an avid reader and student since I was a little girl. I always loved school and generally made good grades. There are some topics about which I've learned a lot over the years. But when I come into God's presence and hold His Word in my hand, I feel deeply needy to learn from Him. Further, I'm in awe that He would stoop to reveal the secrets of His heart to me. Surely such riches are worth whatever time, discipline, and sacrifice are necessary to mine them from His treasure store.

My undergraduate degree is in piano performance. From time to time the university I attended would offer "master classes" in which accomplished pianists would teach the secrets they had acquired over many years of study and performance. Listening to and learning from them was inspiring and an honor. But nothing can compare to the joy and privilege of sitting at the feet of our heavenly Master, learning from Him "in whom are hidden all the treasures of wisdom and knowledge" (Col. 2:3).

MAKE IT PERSONAL

1. What are some inferior motivations you have sometimes had for spending time in the Word and prayer?

2. Think of someone with whom you share a particularly close relationship. What are some of the elements that have contributed to developing and maintaining that friendship?

3. How might those elements apply to cultivating a close relationship with the Lord?

4. Record an instance in which God used His Word to cleanse your heart, to restore your soul, or to teach you something of His ways.

5. Write a brief paragraph expressing why you want to cultivate a consistent devotional life.

6. Read aloud the prayer of David in Psalm 25:4–5. Then pray it back to God in your own words.

CHAPTER 4

The Outer Walk

Are you thirsty for a closer relationship with God? Do you desire to have a heart that is pure and free from sin? Do you need Him to restore your soul each day? Do you want Him to teach you His ways? Thus far, we've looked at four reasons for spending time alone with God on a daily basis—purposes related to our inner life with Him. But He wants to do even more.

We turn now to four other significant purposes—results that will be seen in our walk with Him and others as we sit at His feet and linger in His presence.

SUBMISSION

Through time spent alone with the Lord in His Word and prayer, our lives are brought into alignment with God and His will. For sure, this must be a work of the Spirit, as the idea of yielding to the control or will of another is entirely contrary to our old nature.

When we became children of God, we received a new

nature that recognizes God's right to rule over us and wants to please Him and submit to His will. However, although our spirit wants to obey God, our "flesh" (our natural inclination) wars against our spirit and wants to have its own way.

As a result, we are often tempted to resent, resist, or run from difficult people and circumstances God brings into our lives. In so doing, we end up resisting God Himself.

The problem is that we fail to see the hand of God superintending our lives. He wants to use this trial to train us, to mold us into the image of His Son, and to develop godly character in us.

Left to ourselves, we continue to chafe under the circumstance until we're eaten up with bitterness and resentment. But things change when we enter into God's presence and wait quietly before Him, when we place our lives under the ministry and microscope of His Word. Our resistance is exposed, we see the sovereign purposes of God who is acting for our own good, and we realize the folly of trying to "box" with Him.

As His Spirit works within us, our spirits become pliable and are brought into submission to His authority, and we joyously embrace His will. We begin to thank God for that which once seemed so distasteful to us, knowing that His will is good and that, in His time and in His way, He is able to make the most bitter waters sweet.

Relinquishing Control

Over the years I have walked, wept, and prayed with women through almost every conceivable ordeal, some of which have been unbelievably tragic or complex. Through those experiences I have learned a foundational truth. Whether the problem is earth-shattering or a mere blip on the radar screen of our lives, ultimately, the real issue is this: "Will I surrender to God's hand and purposes in my life?" Those who refuse to relinquish control become emotionally and spiritually bankrupt—bitter, demanding, difficult to live with. On the other hand, those who say in simple surrender, "Yes, Lord," emerge from the experience spiritually rich, and their lives become a source of grace and encouragement to others who are hurting.

Our initial prayer may be, "O Lord, please remove this cup of suffering from me." Then, we are reminded of the Son of God, who was given a bitter cup to drink, full of all the vilest sin of the world. He, too, asked that this cup might be removed from Him, that He might not have to drink it. But He submitted His will to the will of the Father and chose the pathway of the cross, knowing that His obedience would please the Father and bring about the redemption of sinners. In the presence of such costly submission, our hearts are softened, our wills are bent, and we begin to pray, "O Father, not what I will, but what You will. If it pleases You, it pleases me."

Wrestling with God

Jacob was a man with a godly heritage and a future bright with the promises of God. But he was also a man who always seemed to be kicking against the boundaries—never content, always restless, always contending for that which God wanted to give him, but wanting to get it his way.

One day he came to a wall he couldn't move. In a matter of hours, he would have to face his twin brother, whom he had cheated years earlier and who was now coming to meet him accompanied by an army. For the first time in his life, Jacob couldn't manipulate his way around or out of a problem—which was exactly where God wanted him.

In the middle of the night, Jacob finally got alone with the One who had been silently engineering all the circumstances of his life. Just Jacob and God. No one else around. In the stillness of that long night, Jacob wrestled for all he was worth, refusing to give up the struggle—until finally, exhausted, he realized that he would never, ever be able to control God.

His will broken, his hip out of joint (don't expect to wrestle with God and come out unscathed), and his name changed, Jacob (now "Israel") emerged from that divine encounter a new man.

And so will we when we finally get alone with God. In those precious (and sometimes painful) encounters, our lives will undergo a radical adjustment in which our wills become aligned with His. When we emerge, it will be to say with our Savior, "I delight to do your will, O my God" (Ps. 40:8).

Knowing the tendency of my heart to want its own will, I have made it a frequent practice to get on my knees before the Lord. In so doing, I acknowledge that He is my Lord and I am His servant. As I bow before Him physically, my independent, willful self bows to His authority. I lay down my resistance, wave the white flag of surrender, and say in humble submission and worship, "Yes, Your Majesty."

DIRECTION

I have virtually no sense of direction. I would be forever lost without GPS, and it's not unusual for me to get turned around in a hotel and have to ask for help in finding the elevator or the lobby.

Finding God's will regarding our lives, relationships, and responsibilities can be a lot trickier than finding a hotel lobby, a restaurant, or a doctor's office. That's another important reason for spending time alone with Him on a consistent basis.

One of the things I appreciate about my husband and other good friends is the opportunity to ask for their input in areas where they have expertise or experience that I lack. My questions range from such practical issues as whether our furnace needs to be replaced and whether our car and property insurance are adequate, to weightier matters such as the hiring of a new team member and whether I should tackle a specific project.

God desires to have the kind of relationship with us where we are quick to seek His counsel and direction. His Word says, "If any of you lacks wisdom, let him ask God, who gives generously to all without reproach, and it will be given him" (James 1:5).

During our quiet time we enter into His presence and lay our lives before Him—our schedules, our questions, and various circumstances and decisions we're facing. Then, with His Word open before us, we listen and seek to discover His heart on the issue. We wait quietly before Him until He shines His light on our path.

The fact is, we need His guidance on *everything*, big and small. Take the matter of schedule and priorities. I find that when I agree to meetings, appointments, and obligations without first seeking direction from the Lord—I end up with the frustration of having more to do than I can possibly handle, as well as irritation over interruptions that put me further behind.

I've learned how important it is to submit my calendar and daily schedule to the Lord, to ask Him before I make a commitment, to seek His will regarding my priorities, and to ask Him to order every aspect of my day (including the interruptions) according to His will. Then, when those disruptions come (as they will), I can have the wisdom to discern whether they are coming from His hand (in which case they are to be joyfully accepted) or whether they are to be avoided as unnecessary distractions.

Learning to Listen to God

As I read the New Testament accounts of Jesus' life, I'm struck by how touch-sensitive He was to the will of His Father. This particularly comes out in the Gospel of John. Over and over again Jesus spoke of doing the work His Father had sent Him to do. He refused to say anything that His Father had not told Him to say, to go anywhere that His Father had not told Him to go, or to do anything that His Father had not told Him to do (John 5:19, 30; 6:38; 7:16; 8:28; 12:49–50; 14:10). So committed was He to pleasing His Father and to acting in one accord with Him that He was unwilling to step out on His own and act independently.

But how did Jesus know what His priorities were to be on a given day when there was a whole world to be redeemed? When a multitude of needy people was standing at His feet, how did He know when to teach them and when to leave them in order to spend time with His disciples? How did He know who was the one woman in the crowd or the one leper by the side of the road that He was supposed to touch that day? How did He know how to handle each individual situation—whether He was to touch the blind man's eyes or simply to speak to him or to make mud and rub it on his eyes? How did He know that He was supposed to rebuke one group for their unbelief but encourage another man who admitted to struggling with doubts?

The answer takes us back to something we read in chapter 1:

> Very early in the morning, while it was still dark, [Jesus] got up, went out, and made his way to a deserted place; and there he was praying. (Mark 1:35 CSB)

He left the crowds long enough and regularly enough to say, "Father, what do *You* want me to do?"—and to listen for the answer.

At the end of this passage, Jesus' disciples sought Him out and reported that everyone was looking for Him. Jesus' activities of the preceding day were "headline news." He was the most popular program in town. This was a publicist's dream! But Jesus said, "We're not going to stay here. We're going on to the next town."

"Seriously, Jesus? We could stay booked here for at least another month! There are so many people who need You here. Why move on?"

"Because that's what My Father wants Me to do."

How did Jesus know that? Because He'd gotten quiet enough, long enough, to listen to His Father's heart.

Some of us have no clue what God wants us to do with our lives or our days. We can't figure out how to resolve relational conflicts, how to meet the needs of those closest to us, how to reach our neighbors with the gospel, or how to make wise decisions. Could it be that we've not sat still long enough to ask our heavenly Father for direction?

How God Speaks

As we read and meditate on the Word, the indwelling Spirit illuminates it to our understanding and gives us wisdom to apply it to specific areas of our lives.

God uses His Word to help us determine our priorities in different seasons. So when someone comes and says, "Will you lead a small group?" or "sing on the worship team" or "babysit for my kids" or "take over this new project for the company" or whatever, what do you do? You say, "Let me check with the Lord first, and I'll let you know."

But how do you "check with the Lord"? Will He actually tell you whether you should join the worship team or take on the new project?

Probably not. But what He *will* do is use His Word and His Spirit to direct your choices.

I've claimed the promise of Proverbs 16:3 more often than I can count:

> Commit your work to the LORD,
>   and your plans will be established.

As I'm praying regarding a specific decision or issue, I sometimes symbolically place that concern in my hands, then lift my hands up to the Lord and say, "Lord, I'm committing this matter to You. I want to do what You want me to do. Please establish my thoughts and use Your Word to guide me."

God may answer that prayer by bringing to mind Scriptures that have bearing on the situation. He may impress me to seek counsel from a mature, godly friend. He may remind me of another responsibility that I would have to neglect in order to take on a new task. Or He may give me the desire, the faith, and the freedom to step out in a new venture.

Scripture says, "In your light do we see light" (Ps. 36:9). And "the unfolding of your words gives light" (Ps. 119:130). Do you need light for your pathway? Do you need direction for how to raise that child for whom no textbook was ever written? How to deal with a husband who is addicted to pornography? How to respond to that overbearing fellow employee? How to encourage a friend who's going through a crisis? How to care for an aging parent with Alzheimer's? How do you get direction?

"The unfolding of your words gives light."

Inquiring of God

Second Chronicles 20 tells the story about a vast army of Moabites and Ammonites that came together to make war against Judah. We read that King Jehoshaphat was alarmed and "set his face to seek the LORD" (v. 3). Before calling a meeting of the National Defense Council, he called a solemn assembly of the people, inviting them to come and fast and seek the Lord. In his prayer that day, Jehoshaphat laid out the facts before the Lord. He closed his prayer by saying, "We do not know what to do, but our eyes are on you" (v. 12). In answer to that prayer, God dramatically and decisively defeated the enemy, using one of the most unusual battle plans in history.

Many years later, the king of Assyria sent the commander of his army to Jerusalem to publicly humiliate and threaten King Hezekiah (2 Kings 18:17–35). When Hezekiah received news of the incident, he sent messengers to the prophet Isaiah to ask him to pray (19:1–4). Isaiah did pray, and the crisis was averted. A short time later, however, the Assyrian king sent another intimidating message to Hezekiah. What was Hezekiah to do? I love his response:

Hezekiah received the letter from the hand of the messengers and read it; and Hezekiah went up to the house of the LORD and spread it before the LORD. And Hezekiah prayed before the LORD.
(2 Kings 19:14–15)

What is the crisis, the difficulty, the decision you are facing? Spread it out before the Lord, and pray:

Lead me, O LORD, in your righteousness . . .
   make your way straight before me. (Ps. 5:8)

The Good Shepherd promises to guide His sheep in "paths of righteousness" (Ps. 23:3). Believe His Word; He will not fail you.

INTERCESSION

Another purpose of spending time alone with the Lord is that we might intercede on behalf of the needs of others.

As we linger in His presence, we find Him to be a "friend . . . closer than a brother" (Prov. 18:24), a Good Shepherd, a loving Father who delights to meet the needs of His children. We look into His face and find grace and acceptance. We listen to His heart, learn of His ways, and receive His provision and direction for our lives.

Now there comes to our mind a friend who is in need. We would gladly meet that need out of our own supply if we could, but our meager resources are insufficient. Then we remember that there is One whose supply never runs out and who delights to give good gifts to His children. And so we are emboldened to approach Him on behalf of those we care about.

In that quiet time alone with the Lord, we come boldly

and humbly to His throne of grace to obtain mercy not only for ourselves, but for those He has entrusted to our care and whose needs concern us, and to plead for grace to help them in their time of need.

As those four men in Jesus' day tore a hole in the roof to bring their paralyzed friend to the Master (Mark 2:1–5), so we press through whatever barriers of helplessness, doubt, or fear may be in our way in order to lift our friends up to His throne, knowing that He alone can meet their need. There we say, "O Lord, You have done so much for me. Now I come to You again, not for some need of my own—You have abundantly met my needs—but for these ones that I love, asking You to reach down and touch their lives, to make them whole, to win their hearts, to remove the blinders from their eyes, to grant them strength for this hour of testing, to loose them from the chains of sin and rebellion . . ."

"Have You Prayed About It?"

Most of us are born "fixers." Our natural tendency is to take matters into our own hands, to fret and worry, and to demand solutions. In the process we often bypass the most effective means we have of impacting the lives of those around us.

A small plaque on my desk reads, "Have you prayed about it?" Unfortunately I often overlook that simple question until I've already exhausted all my own ideas and solutions.

I'm convinced that if you and I would spend a fraction of the time

> *I'm convinced that if you and I would spend a fraction of the time praying about our concerns for others that we do worrying about them, talking about them to others, and trying to fix them ourselves, we would see a whole lot more results.*

praying about our concerns for others that we do worrying about them, talking about them to others, and trying to fix them ourselves, we would see a whole lot more results. Sometimes I picture God sitting up in heaven, watching us frantically trying to manage everyone else's lives and solve their problems. I imagine Him saying, "Do you want to take care of this? Go ahead. Oh, you want *Me* to handle it? Well, let Me show you what I can do!" The hymn writer was right when he said:

> Oh, what peace we often forfeit,
> Oh, what needless pain we bear,
> All because we do not carry
> Ev'rything to God in prayer![1]

In his wonderful little book *With Christ in the School of Prayer*, Andrew Murray points us to the example of Abraham:

> In Abraham we see how prayer is not only, or even chiefly, the means of obtaining blessing for ourselves, but is the exercise of his royal prerogative to influence the destinies of men, and the will of God which rules them. We do not once find Abraham praying for himself. His prayer for Sodom and Lot, for Abimelech, for Ishmael, prove what power a man, who is God's friend, has to make the history of those around him.[2]

A woman once approached me during a conference where I was ministering and shared that, for many years, she had tried to change her husband. When she had heard me speak a year earlier, she had sensed the Spirit prompting her heart: "Why don't you let Me change you first?" Tenderly she told me how she had allowed God to work in her life and then how she had released her husband to God and begun to really pray for him. With tears of joy in her eyes, she said, "He's not the same man today that he was a year ago!"

Is there someone you've been trying to change? A situation in someone else's life that you've been trying to "fix"? Your truest Friend invites you to bring that needy person to the throne of grace. Enter into His presence and say, "O Lord, I can't meet this child's need; I can't change this person; I can't solve this problem or fix this situation. But I know that nothing is too difficult for You. Please give me wisdom; show me how to be the friend, the wife, the mom, the employee that You want me to be. Please intervene in this person's life. Draw him, draw her, to Yourself."

God doesn't promise to eliminate all our problems or to change all the difficult people in our lives. But He does promise to listen to the cries of His children and to act in accordance with His holy, eternal, loving purposes.

TRANSFORMATION

There's one more purpose of spending time alone with God that I'm eager to mention. It may be the most glorious of all. For as we linger in His presence, we are transformed into His likeness.

You may have heard it said that couples who've been married for years start to look like each other. I don't know how often that's actually the case, but I do know that we become like the people we spend time with. We begin to take on the characteristics of the people and things on which we focus. For example, a woman who becomes fixated on her critical, controlling mother-in-law risks becoming a critical, controlling woman herself. How important it is, then, to fix our eyes on the One whose likeness we wish to bear.

We saw earlier how Moses spent hours and days alone in the presence of God. The Scripture tells us that when Moses came down from receiving God's Law on Mount Sinai, he "did not realize that the skin of his face shone as a result of his speaking with the LORD" (Ex. 34:29 CSB). The manifest glory of God was reflected from Moses' face. The passage goes on to say that

> when Moses had finished speaking with them, he put a veil over his face. But whenever Moses went before the LORD to speak with him, he would remove the veil until he came out. After he came out, he would tell the Israelites what he had been commanded, and the Israelites would see that Moses's face was radiant. Then Moses would put the veil over his face again until he went to speak with the LORD. (Ex. 34:33–35 CSB)

Metamorphosis or Masquerade?

When the apostle Paul wrote to the Corinthians, he referred to this account and explained its significance for our lives. He compared the glory of the old covenant, which faded away and ministered condemnation and death, to the far superior glory of the new covenant, which gives life and will never fade away. Then he explained that, as Moses gazed upon the glory of God with an unveiled face and was transformed by the sight, so "we all, with unveiled face, beholding the glory of the Lord, are being transformed into the same image from one degree of glory to another" (2 Cor. 3:18).

This is a remarkable truth. Paul is saying that as we come into God's presence without masks or pretense, but with our lives open and exposed before Him, and as we steadfastly gaze on Him, we will gradually take on His image—we will be transformed.

The word translated "transformed" is a form of the Greek word *metamorphoó*,[3] the word from which we get our English word *metamorphosis*. It suggests a complete change that takes place from the inside out, much as a caterpillar is metamorphosed into a butterfly. Besides the passage in 2 Corinthians 3, this root word is used in just two other instances in the New Testament. It's used in the Gospels to describe what took place on the Mount of Transfiguration, as Jesus prayed and was "*transfigured* before them, and his face shone like the sun, and his clothes became white as light" (Matt. 17:2; see also Mark 9:29). It's used again in Romans 12:2, where Paul says that we are not to be conformed to this world, but rather, we are to be "transformed" by the renewing of our minds.

In contrast to being transformed, we read in 2 Corinthians 11:13–14 of "false apostles, deceitful workmen, disguising themselves as apostles of Christ," and of Satan himself, who "disguises himself as an angel of light." The word translated "disguise" is the Greek word *metaschēmatizō*,[4] which speaks of change that is merely outward—simply a change of appearance.

This second word is one we could use to describe children dressed up for Halloween as action figures or elves. Those children are not really action figures or elves—they are just wearing a mask or a costume that makes them appear to be something other than what they really are.

The sad fact is that many of us as believers are merely masquerading as "good Christians." Inwardly we're not like Christ at all—we're selfish, lazy, bitter, and angry. But we want everyone to think we're like Jesus, so we put on our "good Christian" masks—especially when we get to church.

When we masquerade in the energy of our own flesh we're likely to end up frazzled and frustrated. God wants us to be metamorphosed—transformed from the inside out, changed into the image of the Lord Jesus.

How does that glorious process take place? As we behold Him "with an unveiled face," as we gaze steadfastly upon His likeness, we will become like Him, by the power of His Holy Spirit. As you spend time each day beholding Jesus in His Word, and listening to His voice, your life will be transfigured from the inside out. You'll begin to think as He thinks, love as He loves, and obey His voice as He obeyed the will of His Father.

> *As you spend time each day beholding Jesus in His Word, and listening to His voice, your life will be transfigured from the inside out.*

Do you want to be a gracious, kind, loving, sweet-spirited woman? You can be, and you will be, as you are transformed in His presence.

And when will that process be complete? When we finally see Him face-to-face, "we shall be like him, because we shall see him as he is" (1 John 3:2).

Transformed by Love

In the Old Testament book called the Song of Solomon (or Song of Songs), we read the story of a handsome, wealthy king who decides to find a bride. Much to everyone's surprise, the king doesn't pick one of the wealthy, educated, well-bred young women of the city. Rather, he goes out into the country and selects a common, ordinary peasant woman to be his bride. She is not beautiful; in fact, her skin is rough and dark from having worked out in the sun in her family's vineyards. When the king brings her back to the palace, the "daughters of Jerusalem" are astonished at his choice. And no one is more astonished than the woman herself.

Nonetheless, the king takes his bride into his bedchamber, where he lavishes his love on her. By the end of the story, this young peasant woman has become a lovely, radiant woman whose beauty attracts the attention of all who see her. What has happened? She has spent time alone with her bridegroom, and she has taken on his characteristics. It is not her own loveliness, but his, that others see in her. She has been transformed by his love.

Deep within the heart of every true child of God is a longing to be like Jesus. But there are no shortcuts to Christlikeness. Shortcuts only lead to masquerading. There is simply no substitute for spending consistent, quality time alone in His presence. If we want to be transformed, we must be willing to do as an old hymn encourages us:

> Take time to be holy,
> Speak oft with thy Lord;
> Abide in Him always,
> And feed on His Word. . . .
>
> Take time to be holy,
> The world rushes on;
> Spend much time in secret
> With Jesus alone;
>
> By looking to Jesus,
> Like Him thou shalt be;
> Thy friends in thy conduct
> His likeness shall see.[5]

MAKE IT PERSONAL

1. Have you been resisting God's choices or will in some area of your life? Will you choose to wave the white flag of surrender and submit your will to His? You may wish to bow physically before Him, then express your heart in words something like these: "Yes, Lord; I receive this as from Your hand. Use it to mold and make me into Your likeness."

2. Is there a concern that is pressing in on you? Why not "spread it out" before the Lord, as Hezekiah did with the threatening letter from the king of Assyria? Find some tangible symbol of that problem (for example, a text, photo, bill, journal entry, or marriage license), lay it before the Lord, and ask Him to give you wisdom, direct your steps, meet the need, and bring glory to Himself through the situation.

3. Record the name of a friend or family member who has a significant need. Summarize the situation. Then purpose to intercede on that person's behalf as the Lord brings them to mind in the days ahead.

4. Make a list of qualities in the life of Jesus that you want to be true in your life. Ask God to transform you into His likeness as you behold Him in His Word.

PART THREE

The Pattern of a Devotional Life

*Very early in the morning,
while it was still dark, [Jesus] got up.*
MARK 1:35 CSB

The morning watch is essential. You must not face the day until you have faced God, nor look into the face of others until you have looked into His. You cannot expect to be victorious, if the day begins only in your own strength.

Face the work of every day with the influence of a few thoughtful, quiet moments with your heart and God. Do not meet other people, even those of your own home, until you have first met the great Guest and honored Companion of your life—Jesus Christ.

Meet Him alone. Meet Him regularly. Meet Him with His open Book of counsel before you; and face the regular and irregular duties of each day with the influence of His personality definitely controlling your every act.

STREAMS IN THE DESERT

CHAPTER 5

Getting Started

Okay, you say. I see the importance of spending time alone with God. I really want to make this a priority in my life. I want to cultivate a relationship with God and be transformed into the image of Christ. But... how do I get started?

In this chapter we'll look at three general principles in relation to establishing a personal devotional life. Each of these principles is taught in Scripture and illustrated in the life of Jesus. Then, in the chapters that follow, we'll consider specific ingredients that are an important part of our time alone with God.

A CONSISTENT PRACTICE

> Jesus often withdrew...
> Luke 5:16 NIV

The first principle is one we've seen earlier in this book. Jesus made time alone with His Father a consistent part of His daily schedule. Can it be any less important for us to do so? But a daily time alone with God in His Word and prayer is not just an obligation; it's an incredible privilege. The God of the universe wants to meet with *us*.

In his helpful book *Spiritual Disciplines for the Christian Life*, Donald Whitney issues this winsome invitation:

> Think of it: The Lord Jesus Christ is willing to meet with you privately for as long as you want; willing—even eager—to meet with you every day! Suppose you had been one of the thousands who followed Jesus around for much of the last three years of His earthly life. Can you imagine how excited you would have been if one of His disciples said, "The Master sent me to tell you that He is willing to meet with you in private whenever you're ready, and for as much time as you want to spend, and He'll be expecting you most every day"? What a privilege! Who would have complained about this expectation? Well, that marvelous privilege and expectation actually does belong to you—today, tomorrow, and always.[1]

I've had the joy of walking with the Lord since early childhood. I have been blessed to grow up in a godly home, to receive fourteen years of Christian education, to be exposed to the lives of many godly men and women, and to sit under some of the best Bible teachers of our generation.

But none of that is enough to sustain my walk with the Lord today. I've come to believe that it's impossible for me to cultivate an intimate relationship with God or to become the woman He wants me to be apart from spending *daily* time alone with Him. As is true in human relationships, I can't set aside time for God sporadically, whenever I'm able to squeeze Him into my schedule, and hope to enjoy a vital, growing friendship with Him.

A Daily Supply

During the forty years that the children of Israel wandered in the wilderness, en route from Egypt to the Promised Land, God provided for all their needs—sometimes in unusual ways. He met their physical need for bread by sending manna, which arrived in the form of "flakes on the desert surface, as fine as frost on the ground" (Ex. 16:14 csb). How often did He send the manna? Every day except the weekly Sabbath. And how often did the people have to gather the manna? Every day except the weekly Sabbath. Six days a week, fifty-two weeks a year, for forty years.

Every person had to gather his or her own portion (v. 16). No one could gather a supply for another. God gave exactly what was needed for all individuals to have their needs met for that day.

This physical "bread" was a picture of the Bread of Life—the Word of God. God created both our bodies and our souls to require daily sustenance. He reminded His people that "man does not live by bread alone, but . . . by every word that comes from the mouth of the Lord" (Deut. 8:3). They needed more than physical nourishment; they needed spiritual nourishment as well. Just as they had to gather and eat physical bread on a daily basis, so they needed the Bread of Life to feed their souls on a daily basis.

When Jesus taught us to pray, "Give us this day our daily bread" (Matt 6:11; Luke 11:3), He was not only teaching us to trust God to supply our daily physical needs, but He was also reminding us of the importance of seeking from Him the spiritual nourishment that our souls need each day.

The nineteenth century preacher D. L. Moody said, "A man can no more take in a supply of grace for the future than he can eat enough for the next six months, or take sufficient air into his lungs at one time to sustain life for a week. We must draw upon God's boundless store of grace from day to day as we need it."[2] That store of grace is made available to us one day at a time, and the manna in the wilderness reminds us of our need to gather it up for ourselves, one day at a time.

Daily Routines

The Old Testament tabernacle had numerous reminders of our need for daily communion with God. At the entrance to the Holy of Holies (the inner sanctuary that only the high priest could enter) stood the altar of incense. God told Moses:

> Aaron shall burn on it sweet incense every morning; when he tends the lamps, he shall burn incense on it. And when Aaron lights the lamps at twilight, he shall burn incense on it, a perpetual incense before the LORD throughout your generations. (Ex. 30:7–8 NKJV)

The incense that was offered on this altar spoke of the praise and prayers of a redeemed people ascending to God. It was to be offered up, not occasionally, or whenever the priest happened to think of it, but every day—every morning and every night.

Why did it matter to God if His people occasionally missed a day or two of lighting incense? Because He was pursuing a relationship with them and He knew that required consistent, daily communication. And so we are invited to enter into His holy presence, taking with us the incense of praise and prayer daily offered up to God.

There were other regular routines that took place in the

tabernacle. The oil lamps had to be kept burning continually, sacrifices had to be made, the showbread (special loaves on a special table—see Num. 4:7) had to be replaced, and the priests had to be cleansed—every morning, every evening, day in, day out.

Could those activities eventually become mindless routines that held no meaning for the people? Absolutely. In fact, that's exactly what happened to the Israelites. They lost sight of the purpose behind the routines—to walk with their God. But the routines were established by God. And they were necessary to nurture and sustain a relationship with Him.

There's always a danger that a daily quiet time or any other spiritual discipline can deteriorate into a lifeless routine. But I've discovered that it's much easier to breathe life back into an existing routine than to get life where there is no routine at all.

> *It's much easier to breathe life back into an existing routine than to get life where there is no routine at all.*

The Bridegroom Desires His Bride

As you set aside time each day to meet with God, don't forget that the objective is to cultivate an intimate relationship between you and God. He longs for such a relationship with you, and He is eager to spend that time with you.

There is a touching moment in the Song of Solomon when the king asks his bride to join him so they can spend time alone together. From outside the window he calls to her,

> Rise up, my love, my fair one,
> And come away....
> Let me see your face,

Let me hear your voice;
For your voice is sweet,
And your face is lovely." (Song 2:10, 14 NKJV)

Realizing that my heavenly Bridegroom longs to spend time with me has reshaped my perspective on the whole matter of daily devotions. Time with Him is not just something *I* need (though I do need Him desperately); it's also something that fulfills a longing in *His* heart. When we come before Him each day, we want to see His face and hear His voice. But have you ever stopped to realize that He wants to see *our* face and hear *our* voice?

After all these years of walking with Him, I still can't fathom why He would want to meet with me. But I know it's true. So when I enter into His presence, it's with the thought that He wants to be with me and that I can bring Him pleasure by letting Him see my face and hear my voice.

In the light of eternity, spending time with God is more necessary than anything else you or I do on a daily basis, including eating, sleeping, getting dressed, and going to work.

At this particular season of your life (and remember that seasons do change), you may not be able to spend lengthy, uninterrupted time alone with the Lord every day. But if knowing God and having a relationship with Him is important to you, you can determine to set aside *some* time each day to listen to Him and to let Him know that you love Him and need Him.

IN THE MORNING

Very early in the morning, while it was still dark . . .
Mark 1:35 CSB

Whenever the subject of daily devotions comes up, the suggestion of meeting the Lord "in the morning" can be a sticking point or a guilt inducer—especially for those who don't consider themselves "morning people" or whose family or work responsibilities make this difficult. In teaching on the personal devotional life, I've often been tempted to minimize or skip over this point. But the more I study the Word and the ways of God, the more convinced I am of the value of making the effort to start our day (whenever that may be) with Him.

In addition to Jesus' pattern, we find many other examples throughout Scripture that highlight the significance of meeting God in the morning.

When God called Moses up onto Mount Sinai, He directed Him to "be ready *in the morning*, and come up *in the morning* . . . and present yourself to Me there" (Ex. 34:2 NKJV).

God sent manna for His people *in the morning*. The day's supply of nourishment was to be gathered *in the morning*, while it was still fresh.

David clearly rose early in the morning for worship, prayer, and meditation—as evidenced repeatedly in the Psalms:

> My voice You shall hear in the morning, O LORD;
> In the morning I will direct it to You,
> And will look up. (Ps. 5:3 NKJV)

> But I, O LORD, cry to you;
>   in the morning my prayer comes before you. (Ps. 88:13)

> Wake up, my soul!
> Wake up, harp and lyre!
> I will wake up the dawn.
> I will praise you, Lord. (Ps. 57:8–9 CSB)

> I rise before dawn and cry for help;
> I hope in your words. (Ps. 119:147)

> Let me hear in the morning of your steadfast love. (Ps. 143:8)

Centuries later the prophet Isaiah testified to a similar practice:

> He awakens me each morning;
> He awakens my ear to listen like those being instructed. (Isa. 50:4 CSB)

And Jeremiah praised God that His faithful love and mercies are "new every morning" (Lam. 3:23).

Think about that. Every morning God has a fresh store of mercies available for you and me. When we don't take time in the morning to gather what He has provided for that day, we're saying, in essence, *I can make it through this day on my own. My strength, my wisdom, my resources are sufficient for the demands of this day.* Not only do we forfeit the grace of God, but our self-sufficiency and pride result in Him resisting us throughout the day.

You may be wondering, *Just how early in the morning do I need to meet with God?* I don't know what time early is for you. "Early" for my sweet husband feels like the middle of the night for me! Early for me is before I begin handling emails or tackling other tasks awaiting me on my phone or laptop. If I don't meet with God before then, it becomes difficult for me to find a quiet time, a quiet place, or a quiet heart for the rest of the day. After that point my quiet time will likely be fragmented at best.

That doesn't mean that to be spiritual you have to be one of those women who just loves mornings and bounds out of bed two hours before the sun comes up. Neither am I suggesting a legalistic mindset that says you must be on your knees by a certain time in the morning. Don't forget that the purpose of a quiet time is to know God and to have a relationship with Him, not to follow a set of rules. But if you and I want to be like Jesus, if we want to really know God, it's worth paying the price to get out of bed in the morning to seek His face.

Men and women of God throughout history have stressed the importance of meeting God in the morning. Listen to the unison urging of these spiritual greats:

> Do not have your concert first and tune your instruments afterward. Begin the day with God. (J. Hudson Taylor)[3]

> It is a good rule never to look into the face of man in the morning till you have looked into the face of God. (Charles H. Spurgeon)[4]

> The best time to converse with God is before worldly occasion stands knocking at the door to be let in: the morning is, as it were, the cream of the day; let the cream be taken off, and let God have it. Wind up thy heart towards heaven in the beginning of the day, and it will go the better all the day after. He that loseth his heart in the morning in the world, will hardly find it again all the day. (Thomas Watson)[5]

One of the things I've learned over the years is that success in meeting God in the morning begins the night before. Each evening we make choices that determine how we start the next day. One of the reasons my dad was able to be so consistent at spending at least an hour with God at the beginning of each day was that he was disciplined about getting to

> Success in meeting God in the morning begins the night before.

bed the night before. Regardless of what was going on in our home, no later than ten o'clock he would excuse himself and prepare to be in bed by eleven.

Today my siblings and I laugh affectionately when we recall hearing our dad say to guests, "Good night, everyone! Be sure to lock the door and turn out the lights when you leave." He didn't communicate a rigid or uptight spirit about this discipline. He just wanted to be sure he didn't miss the most important appointment of his day—an early morning meeting with the most important Person in his life. How blessed I've been by the example of Art DeMoss, along with that of my precious husband, whose consistent practice is remarkably similar.

Today we have more ways to fritter away late night hours than my father possibly could have imagined—to the detriment of our happiness and well-being. Rather than staying up at night gaming or scrolling mindlessly through our social media feeds, how much better off would our souls be, how much more content, less distracted, and better rested would we be, if we got to bed earlier and even spent the last portion of our evening listening to godly music or meditating on Scripture—preparing for our morning appointment with God.

By the way, you can't imagine the impact it will have on your children if they know when they awaken that you've already met with the Lord—that you've prayed for them and committed the day's activities to the Lord. To this day, whenever I'm tempted to hit my day running (as is often the case), I have the image of parents who set the pattern of spending time with the Lord as the first business of their day.

Over the years God has used this old-time poem by Ralph Spaulding Cushman to encourage me to meet Him in the morning:

> I met God in the morning
>   When my day was at its best,
> And His presence came like sunrise,
>   Like a glory in my breast.
>
> All day long the presence lingered,
>   All day long, He stayed with me,
> And we sailed in perfect calmness
>   O'er a very troubled sea.
>
> Other ships were blown and battered,
>   Other ships were sore distressed,
> But the winds that seemed to drive them
>   Bring to us a peace and rest.
>
> Then I thought of other mornings,
>   With a keen remorse of mind,
> When I too had loosed the moorings,
>   With the presence left behind.
>
> So I think I know the secret,
>   Learned from many a troubled way:
> You must seek Him in the morning,
>   If you want Him through the day![6]

A SOLITARY PLACE

> Jesus went out to a solitary place.
> Luke 4:42 NIV

In order to cultivate growing oneness and intimacy, husbands and wives need to spend time alone with each other—away from other friends, acquaintances, and even their own children. The same is true of sustaining an intimate relationship with the Father.

Jesus understood this well. Luke 5:15 tells us that when news about Him spread, "great crowds gathered to hear him and to be healed of their infirmities." Jesus had compassion on the multitudes and gave of Himself sacrificially to minister to their needs. But He knew He could not meet their needs apart from His relationship with His Father. So the very next verse tells us that Jesus often "withdrew to *deserted places* and prayed" (v. 16 CSB).

When God called Moses up to meet with Him on Mount Sinai, He said, "Present yourself there to me on the top of the mountain. *No one shall come up with you*" (Ex. 34:2–3). As part of a community of faith, we need times to worship, pray, and seek the Lord in the company of God's people. But we must also have times that are set apart to be alone with Him.

A Tent of Meeting

Before the tabernacle was constructed, we're told that Moses used to take a tent and pitch it outside the camp some distance away, calling it the "tent of meeting." This meeting place was set up away from the crowd, away from the normal flow of traffic, a special place reserved for those who wished to meet and "consult" with Yahweh (Ex. 33:7).

I've found it helpful to set apart in my home a place for meeting with God. For many years, I would retreat to a comfortable chair in a corner of my study. That chair became my tent of meeting, a place I went to meet with God. When that chair became threadbare after decades of use, I replaced it with another one. And when I'm away from home, wherever I may be, I seek to establish a tent of meeting in my heart—

a quiet place, a solitary place, a place away from the crowd, where I can be alone with God.

A mom with littles may find it difficult to find a solitary place, but with some ingenuity it can happen. A friend shared with me how she managed to withdraw from the crowd:

> I have a sweet memory of our son, Jon, when he was approximately eighteen months old. He would get out of his baby bed each morning, coming to find me. The only place in our small house where I could be away from the children (ages eight, six, two, and one) was in our small bathroom with a sliding door. Of course, there was only one place to sit in the bathroom. So, with the lid down and my Bible open I'd have my quiet time. Jon would come outside the door, put his little hand under the door, and hold on to my foot until I finished. At that early age, he had learned that I had to read my Bible daily.

Another friend with small children once said to me, "There have been times when we have been visiting relatives and I've had to have my quiet time by a night-light in the same room where my children were sleeping. I've found that there's a way to do it if you really want to."

Your tent of meeting may be a bathroom, a closet, a hallway, or your vehicle. The important thing is that you find a place where you can meet *alone* with your heavenly Bridegroom.

Some people find it difficult to get used to solitude, especially if they're accustomed to always being around other people or listening to music, news, sports, or their favorite podcasts day and night. Being quiet and alone with God can be an adjustment and a discipline. But as one writer of a past era reminds us:

> There is a strange strength conceived in solitude.
> Crows go in flocks and wolves in packs, but the lion

and the eagle are solitaires.
> Strength is not in bluster and noise. Strength is in quietness. The lake must be calm if the heavens are to be reflected on its surface. Our Lord loved the people, but how often we read of His going away from them for a brief season....
>
> The one thing needed above all others today is that we shall go apart with our Lord, and sit at His feet in the sacred privacy of His blessed presence. Oh, for the lost art of meditation! Oh, for the culture of the secret place! Oh, for the tonic of waiting upon God![7]

A Personal Testimony (One Happy Meal to Go, Please!)

From the time I was twenty, for nearly a dozen years, I traveled full-time, year-round, in ministry. During that period I became a fast-food junkie. More times than I care to remember, I picked up my tacos or burger and fries at a drive-through window and then sat in the parking lot for the few minutes it took to inhale my meal. Frequently I didn't even bother to stop the car, but just keep going, eating my lunch while driving to the next thing on my schedule.

I actually didn't mind living that way—until I turned thirty. About that time my body started to feel the effects of those years of junk food. I found that my body was craving a more nutritious, balanced diet and that I couldn't keep eating the way I had for more than a decade. I had to make some significant changes in my lifestyle to accommodate my body's needs.

Some years later, I faced an even more significant "health crisis." After going through an eighteen-month period in which my schedule had been unusually grueling, I woke up one day and realized that I had become a *spiritual* fast-food junkie.

I had allowed deadlines, projects, and demands to take priority over my relationship with the Lord. Oh, I still had a quiet time—of sorts. I usually managed to get in some sort of spiritual meal. But all too frequently that meal had come to consist of hurriedly reading a short passage of Scripture just before running out the door to accomplish one more thing for God.

Spiritually, I was living in fast-food drive-throughs. I was having my devotions, if you could call it that. But I wasn't having *devotion*. I wasn't meeting with God. I wasn't nurturing our relationship. Like the young bride depicted in the Song of Solomon, I had tended the "vineyards" of others but had failed to care for the garden of my own heart (Song 1:6). As God used circumstances to reveal my malnourished spiritual condition, I began to realize what a price I had paid for those months of neglect.

How grateful I am for a merciful, long-suffering heavenly Father who never stops pursuing a love relationship with His children. Graciously, kindly, He wooed my heart that had become distracted and desensitized to Him. His goodness led me to repent of having wandered so far from His side, to renew my vows to Him, and to reestablish my relationship with Him as the number one priority of my day. As I responded to His initiative, the Good Shepherd began the process of restoring my soul, leading me to the still waters and green pastures that I so desperately needed.

In the Song of Solomon we are told of an instance when the bride failed to respond to the initiative of her bridegroom and experienced a loss of intimacy. Troubled by the breach in the relationship, she set out on an intense search for her beloved. In recounting that thrilling moment when he was restored to her, she says,

> I found him whom my soul loves.
> I held him, and would not let him go. (Song 3:4)

There have been other lapses in my devotion to Christ in the years since. But each time the Lord has been faithful to renew my longing for Him and restore my soul. What a joy to be able to say with that grateful bride, "I have found Him whom my soul loves." My heart's desire is to hold fast to Him and not to let Him go—to experience unbroken fellowship with Him and to make a conscious, deliberate choice to spend time alone with Him each day.

MAKE IT PERSONAL

1. Which of the three elements of a quiet time discussed in this chapter (a consistent practice, in the morning, a solitary place) do you find the most difficult?

2. Have you ever had a season when you found yourself taking shortcuts in your devotional life—living in a spiritual fast-food drive-through? Describe that time and some of the consequences you experienced in your relationship with the Lord and others.

3. What are the greatest barriers you encounter in trying to maintain a consistent time alone with the Lord in the morning?

    Ask the Lord what practical steps you could take to overcome those obstacles. Record any insights He gives you.

4. If you have not already established a consistent habit of meeting alone with the Lord, would you purpose to spend some time in the Word and prayer each morning for the next seven days? Share your commitment with a friend.

PART FOUR

The Problems of a Devotional Life

I sought him, but found him not.
SONG OF SOLOMON 3:1

I throw myself down in my chamber, and I call in, and invite God, and his angels thither, and when they are there, I neglect God and his angels, for the noise of a fly, for the rattling of a coach, for the whining of a door; I talk on, in the same posture of praying; Eyes lifted up; knees bowed down; as though I prayed to God; and, if God, or his angels should ask me, when I thought last of God in that prayer, I cannot tell.

JOHN DONNE

CHAPTER 6

"The Hard Thing for Me Is…"

When I first set out to write this book, I developed a questionnaire asking women for their input. It included such questions as:

- Why do you believe it's important to have a daily quiet time? (Out of 178 women who responded, 175 indicated they felt it was "very important" to have a consistent, daily quiet time with the Lord.)
- What are some of the benefits you've received from having a regular quiet time?
- What have you found to be the greatest obstacle(s) to a consistent, meaningful devotional life?
- What insights would you share with others about how to have a meaningful devotional life?

Many wrote honestly of their struggles in trying to establish a daily quiet time. And lots of them many made excellent, practical suggestions, some of which I'll share in this chapter.

(Responses to the questionnaire appear in italics throughout the chapter.) I've selected ten of the most common barriers they identified. Perhaps you've found yourself thinking (or saying) some of these at one time or another . . .

"I just can't find the time!"

By far, this was the number one obstacle women shared. Here are just two of many examples:

> *Six years ago I was single and could focus on the Lord. Now that I've been married for three years and have two small children, it's so hard for me to find that time. Please help!*

> *Ten- to twelve-hour workdays take their toll. I don't know how to slow down. How do you make life less hectic?*

> **If you and I don't make a conscious, deliberate effort to set aside time to be with the Lord, other things will always demand our attention.**

The fact is, if you and I don't make a conscious, deliberate effort to set aside time to be with the Lord, other things will always demand our attention. One of my spiritual mentors, now with the Lord, used to say: "Don't try to squeeze God into an already overcrowded schedule. Determine your schedule around Him!" Several of the women we heard from echoed this observation. They suggested making an appointment with God and keeping it as we would any other type of appointment.

Others commented on the necessity of viewing this time as the most important thing in our lives:

> *Don't look at prayer and Bible study as something you try to make time for. Look at it as a need—a need that, if not met, could have serious consequences.*

> • *Our time with the Lord is the most important part of our day. We need to schedule that time, or it won't happen.*

William Gurnall was a devout minister in England during the seventeenth century. He considered it unthinkable that we would be unable to find time to read the Book in which God has communicated His love and grace:

> Could God find heart and time to pen and send this love-letter to thee, and thou find none to read and peruse it! The sick man no time to look on his physician's prescription! The condemned malefactor to look on his prince's letter of grace, wherein a pardon is signed![1]

If you and I want to cultivate a healthy, growing relationship with the Lord, we need His wisdom to decide which activities we should (and should not) say yes to in each season of our lives.

The same is true for families. I've observed many well-meaning parents who live in a whirlwind from morning till night, running themselves and their kids from one event to another. The "activity addiction" this can create in parents and kids alike diminishes their appetite for the Word of God and prayer and makes it difficult to seek Him with a quiet heart.

All activities—whether our own or our children's—must be evaluated in light of ultimate, eternal values. Here's how one woman put it:

> • *It's worth it to put all else aside for a quiet time with God. The laundry will wait. Time with the Lord is of eternal value. In the light of eternity, what difference will all these things make?*

- *This mindset means limiting (or even eliminating) activities that hinder us from putting Him first.*

At one point many years ago, I was faced with just such a decision. I was single and lived alone at the time and found myself turning the television on when I got home at night, mainly for the noise and companionship. But I knew that precious hours were being expended on mindless activity—hours that might have been used to nurture my spirit or to minister to the needs of others. Then I wondered why I couldn't find the time I wanted and needed to spend alone with the Lord.

In my heart I knew my spiritual life would be better off if I didn't have the TV on. Eventually that led to a commitment not to watch television when I was alone—a choice that proved to be one of the best I've ever made. Not only did I have more hours to devote to my relationship with the Lord, but the more time I spent in His presence, the more I wanted to be with Him and the less interested I was in things of this world that just didn't matter.

I've had to say no to other activities as well over the years—even some good, wholesome ones, but none of them as important as sitting at the feet of Jesus and listening to His Word. Today the temptation for me is no longer with the TV, but with my smartphone that is rarely more than inches away and can sap even more time and spiritual vitality with endless, empty activity.

Many of the women who responded to my questionnaire affirmed the importance of:

- *Choose to do it! Do we really believe that meeting with God is as important and necessary as our daily physical food? Then choose to make it a priority!*

- *I've found that if I make time, the Lord will give me time for other things.*

The seventeenth-century preacher Lewis Bayly was plainspoken in urging his hearers to make choices in this life that they would be glad to have made in the next:

> But it may be thou wilt say, that thy business will not permit thee so much time, as to read every morning a chapter. O man, remember that they life is but short, and that all this business is but for the use of this short life; but salvation or damnation is everlasting! Rise up, therefore, every morning by so much time the earlier: defraud they foggy flesh of so much sleep; but rob not thy soul of her food, nor God of His service; and serve the Almighty duly whilst thou hast time and health.[2]

John Piper, a contemporary author and preacher, put it more succinctly but no less directly:

> One of the great uses of Twitter and Facebook will be to prove at the Last Day that prayerlessness was not from lack of time.[3]

"My time with the Lord often seems hurried."

- *In the morning I'm rushed; in the evening, I'm tired and can't concentrate.*

I've come to believe that hurry is one of the deadliest enemies of an effective devotional life. As great a man of God as Martyn Lloyd-Jones had to fight the tendency to hurry God:

> One day recently I wanted to thank God in a certain matter; but at the time I also had business in hand which needed urgent attention. I was on the point of offering up a hurried word of thanksgiving to God in order that I might turn to the urgent task; but realizing what was happening I suddenly said to myself: "That is not the way to thank God. Do you realize whom you are about to thank?" Everything must be laid aside when you are turning to Him; everything, everyone, all things, however urgent. What are they compared to Him? Stop! Pause! Wait! Recollect! Realize what you are doing.[4]

One day many years ago, I was walking on the treadmill while listening to an interview with Henry Blackaby (author of *Experiencing God*) about his personal devotional life. Dr. Blackaby said something in that conversation that profoundly impacted my own time with the Lord.

He told of a time in the past when he had found himself getting up each morning to meet with the Lord, but having to rush that time in order to attend to the various responsibilities of the day. He shared how God had convicted him that it was a grievous offense to "hurry the God of the universe," and how he had determined to move his quiet time up a half hour earlier so he would not be rushed. He'd done so but found that he still ended up being hurried, so he'd moved the time up by another half hour. Dr. Blackaby said, "I kept moving the time up in the morning until I knew that I could meet with God as long as He wanted to meet with me, without being hurried."

As I heard those words from a busy man who evidenced a deep, steady, fruitful walk with God, I purposed in my heart to do whatever was necessary to secure unhurried time to let God speak to me on a daily basis. I've had to make adjustments in my schedule and even make some "sacrifices." But to the extent I've done what is necessary to spend unhurried time with Him, the fruit has been precious and sweet.

"How do I deal with interruptions and distractions?"

> *I sit down with my Bible, read a sentence, the phone rings, the dryer goes off, the TV my husband is watching is too loud ...*

My picture is in the dictionary next to the word "distractible." In fact, in the last few hours since I began working on this chapter, I have fought a steady stream of distractions. A loud utility truck pulled up on the street outside my window and sat there for some thirty minutes—I got up and closed the window so I could concentrate. I got thirsty and went to the kitchen to get something to drink. I got cold and went upstairs to put on warmer clothes. I stopped to check my email messages, which led to tending to several tasks that had nothing to do with this book. I got up to get rid of a spider that I noticed climbing up the wall. Finally I was so tired I had to lie down for a nap! (As I was writing this paragraph, I managed to create yet another distraction by accidentally deleting everything I had written on my laptop in the last fifteen minutes.)

All these distractions took place when no one else was in the house. When you add in hungry or cranky children, barking dogs, texts, phone calls, and repairmen at the door, it can be incredibly difficult to concentrate on Bible reading and prayer.

There will always be possible distractions, but here are a few thoughts that have been helpful to me.

Many distractions can be avoided simply by getting up earlier. We have seen that it was Jesus' practice to get up before daybreak to spend unhurried time with His Father before the crowds began to press in on Him. As I've already mentioned, once emails and texts begin showing up on my phone, I know it's going to be more difficult for me to get a quiet heart before the Lord.

Ask God to help you recognize and ignore unnecessary distractions. For example, I've had to learn that I don't have to answer every phone call, respond to every text message, or check my email every time I get a notification.

Many years ago, I had the honor of meeting with President Ronald Reagan. Out of respect for the man and his position, I would not have considered taking a phone call during that meeting. When I'm in staff meetings or visiting with friends, I generally ignore phone calls except for my husband or emergencies. Yet how often have I found myself in the middle of an appointment with the King of the universe while reflexively responding to random texts as if they were more important than He! Is it not disrespectful for me to put God "on hold" while I stop to attend to every detail that comes my way? Not to speak of how my mind is fragmented and my soul is impoverished as a result.

Be flexible in responding to "divine interruptions." Have you ever found yourself in the middle of reading the Word or praying, only to respond impatiently to a child, a mate, or a friend who interrupts you with a genuine need?

Even Jesus had His quiet time interrupted. In the passage we've already examined in Mark 1, Jesus was interrupted by His disciples coming and telling Him, "Everyone is looking for you!" (v. 37 CSB). Because He had been listening to His Father, He was able to discern when an interruption was God-sent. In this case Jesus realized it was time to go and preach in the nearby villages. Because He was sensitive to the Father, He could respond to interruptions without becoming irritable.

"When I try to read or pray, my mind wanders. I can't concentrate."

When it comes to my own quiet time, many of the distractions are not external, but internal. I no sooner sit down in my "quiet time chair" than I begin thinking of a whole host of things I need to do—thank-you notes to be written, calls to be made, supplies to be ordered, tasks to be completed at work. ... I often even get a sudden, new burden for housecleaning!

The seventeenth-century English poet and preacher John Donne expressed this tendency, so familiar to anyone who has ever sought to set his or her heart on things above:

> A memory of yesterday's pleasures, a fear of tomorrow's dangers, a straw under my knee, a noise in mine ear, a light in mine eye, an any thing, a nothing, a fancy, a chimera in my brain, troubles me in my prayer.[5]

I have found that it often takes preparation to get a quiet heart before the Lord. You may want to start your time with the Lord by singing some worshipful choruses or reading aloud a psalm of praise, asking the Lord to settle your heart in His presence.

When unrelated thoughts or tasks come to mind, rather than stopping to attend to them at the moment or trying to remember them until later, try jotting them down on a notepad. In fact, rather than fighting those thoughts, as you write them down they can become direction for specific prayer. I find that as I place those concerns before the Lord, He gives me wisdom and insight I need to deal with those matters, as well as helping me to organize my to-do list for the day.

Some of the women I surveyed shared that praying aloud while they were out walking helped them stay focused on the Lord. Reading Scripture aloud, recording insights from the Word in a journal, and writing out your prayers are other practices that can help increase concentration.

"What if I have young children?"

- *How do you maintain a quality devotional life when you have younger children whose radar goes off the minute you get out of bed?*

The physical and emotional demands on moms with littles are real. If you've been through that stage or are in it now, you know what it is to feel like you're forever in survival mode. And that's why finding ways to pull away to spend time with Jesus is as important for women in that season as in any other. It can be a lifeline for their hearts (and their sanity), a means of receiving the grace they so desperately need to make it through each day.

I asked a number of mature, godly women how they managed to have consistent devotions when their children were young. Some admitted that they hadn't; most acknowledged that it was not easy; but all agreed that it mattered and was worth the effort and creativity required to make it possible. Here are some practical ideas they shared that you may find helpful if you're in this season.

- *Moms may have to yield their right to a picture-perfect quiet time and realize they can meet the Lord even while they meet physical and emotional needs for their family. Sometimes, when I've read only a few verses, but I've been obedient that* day with my time, and my heart attitudes have honored Christ, I am more content than when I dutifully "check off" my quiet time but have spent the day in my own abilities, resentful of the demands on my time. (A mother of eight)

- The only way I've been able to have consistent devotions with small children is to get up before they do. This season of life does not always lend itself to longer, in-depth study of the Word, but even a few verses and a short prayer and worship time have helped me through many days. God understands our circumstances and our heart's desire to meet with Him. We can't put ourselves on a guilt trip at this stage of life when we can't spend as much time as we'd like in the Word. But it must still be our top priority, however brief it may be.

- Ask God to protect those times. Children can be taught that this is a priority and to leave Mom alone unless there's an emergency. I got up earlier than they got up. I spent time with God during their naps. Later I spent time with God right after they left for school.

- When our daughter was two to three years old, we had a clock that gave the time every thirty minutes. I would tell her that I was having time with Jesus. She would sit with her book (upside down sometimes) and have her quiet time. After the bird cuckooed the next thirty minutes, we would have mom-daughter time. She knew to let me have that time between cuckoos!

- You have to be determined and creative. I remember many times during those early years rocking a sick child in my arms and bouncing another on my feet, while listening to an audio Bible and praying, "Lord, give me something to encourage my soul."

- Remember that this season will not last forever. It's important to maintain our personal time with the Lord during these years. However, the time and place may vary. We must find it when and where we can. God loves us and understands our

> needs. *He will faithfully meet us as we faithfully seek His face. When my children were small, I posted verses on cabinets and over the sink, even on the dash of the car. This made Scripture memorization and meditation so much easier.*
>
> - *It may not be easy, but if you really want to meet with God, you will find a way to do it!*

I've read that Susannah Wesley, mother of nineteen (!) children (nine of whom died in infancy), managed to spend an hour in the morning, an hour in the evening, and often an hour at noon alone with the Lord. Her children learned early that time alone with God was a sacred necessity. Little wonder, then, that two of her sons, John and Charles, grew up to become mighty servants in the kingdom of Christ.

Mothering little ones (or older ones, for that matter) is not for the faint of heart. Your "quiet time" may not be as "quiet" or provide the luxury of as much uninterrupted "time" as in other seasons of life. But this can be a season of leaning on Christ, learning from Him, and finding in Him and His Word just what you need to fill your soul and to invest in the lives He has entrusted to your care.

"I'm so exhausted that I don't have the energy to have a quiet time."

> - *As a single parent I have so little energy. My day starts early, and by the end of the day, I am fatigued. I often have to stop my devotional reading because my eyes won't stay open and I don't know what I've just read.*

Jesus' disciples knew all about being too tired to pray. At the moment that their dearest Friend needed them to keep spiritual watch with Him, they found themselves so emotionally and physically exhausted that they succumbed to sleep. Jesus did not berate them. But He did remind them that the failure to "watch and pray" would leave them vulnerable to temptation.

I've discovered that the more tired I am, the more I need the refreshing of His presence. Yes, there are those days when the eyelids are heavy. But there's something energizing about time spent in the Word, praise, and prayer. Perhaps that's because when we express our weakness and need to God, He lavishes His grace on us.

Look for creative ways to wake up and stay awake. Get out of bed (for me, staying in bed is a sure way to fall asleep). Take a shower. Stand or walk to pray. Sing. If the weather allows, you may want to have your quiet time outside.

If you're consistently exhausted, ask yourself, "Why am I tired?" Is there a medical or physical explanation? (Exercise is close to the top of my "least favorite things to do" list. But when it's part of my regular routine, I find I have greater physical stamina and strength to seek the Lord and to fulfill the responsibilities He has given to me.) Are you making unwise choices with your schedule that are contributing to your weariness? Are you doing some things that aren't on God's agenda for your life at this season?

You may be in a season of life that is unusually draining—during a pregnancy, after the birth of a child, following major surgery, or while caring for an aging parent. If so, don't let the enemy convince you that your tiredness is a spiritual problem, and don't let him use your tiredness as an excuse for not seeking the Lord.

One day a young mother sought me out for counsel. She had just had her fourth child and was disturbed that she had no desire for the Word or prayer. She felt guilty and was even wondering if perhaps she was not a Christian at all. Of course, only the Holy Spirit could give her assurance of salvation, but as I listened, it seemed to me that most of what she was experiencing was likely the result of physical exhaustion due to nursing an infant and inadequate sleep.

Rather than put her on a further guilt trip, I shared with her one of my favorite Old Testament names for God: El Shaddai. Our English Bibles translate that Hebrew name as "Almighty God" or the "All-Sufficient One." But the root word for El Shaddai is the word *shad*, the Hebrew word for "breast." This name pictures God as the "breasted One." Much as a nursing mother pours herself out to satisfy the thirst of her infant, causing the fretful child to be calmed at the mother's breast, so El Shaddai "pours Himself into believing lives"[6] and satisfies His children's thirsty, fretful hearts.

I encouraged that frazzled young mother to meditate on El Shaddai, even as she nursed her infant in the night hours, and to allow the Lord to satisfy and fill her with His unconditional love. As we prayed together, I asked Him to hold this precious woman close to Himself and to pour Himself into her life. At that moment she began to cry—tears of release—as the Holy Spirit ministered grace to her heart and by faith she received the tender love of El Shaddai.

> When your body is bone-weary, ask God for the physical and emotional strength necessary to do His will; He knows your needs and can be trusted to meet them.

When your body is bone-weary, ask God for the physical and emotional strength necessary to do His will; He knows your needs and can be trusted to meet them. In Jesus' time of greatest need, as He prayed in the garden of Gethsemane, Luke's account tells us that "there appeared to him an angel from heaven, strengthening him" (Luke 22:43). He will strengthen you in your weariness, as well, as you rely on Him.

"Sometimes I feel like I'm having my quiet time just out of duty."

- *My quiet time seems to have become legalistic—something to check off my to-do list each day. I feel if I really loved the Lord I would jump out of bed and run to spend time with Him.*

We need to remember that our feelings are not always a reliable gauge of reality. Further, there is value in maintaining any good habit, even when it is not motivated by warm feelings or intense desire. And over time, faithfully carrying out a discipline will often result in greater desire. Our heart's devotion for Him will deepen and grow as we choose to put Him first and invest time in that relationship, regardless of how we may feel.

Several of the women I surveyed spoke from experience about how God blesses us when we make right choices:

- *Sometimes, when we just do it out of obedience, then our hearts are drawn to Him in devotion.*

- *Even when it feels like a duty, even when I seem to be just going through the motions, even when it doesn't feel meaningful, God's blessings come from the quiet times.*

- *I've been praying daily for three years. It started out of duty and I just followed the "steps." But now that our relationship has been established, my quiet times are definitely out of devotion.*

Nineteenth century "Prince of Preachers" Charles Spurgeon encouraged people to pray whether or not they felt like it:

> We should pray when we are in a praying mood, for it would be sinful to neglect so fair an opportunity. We should pray when we are not in the proper mood, for it would be dangerous to remain in so unhealthy a condition.[7]

"How do you handle dry spells?"

- *What has happened when the Bible becomes dry and boring—especially when it used to be so wonderful? Why did I lose my desire?*

Psalm 42 (along with its companion Psalm 43) reads like the journal of a believer in the throes of a spiritual dry spell, and as such, provides us with a model of how to weather our own. The psalmist cries out,

> My soul thirsts for God,
>   for the living God.
> When shall I come and appear before God? . . .
> Why are you cast down, O my soul,
>   and why are you in turmoil within me? (vv. 2, 5)

In the midst of this spiritual desert, he first *looks back* and remembers the joy he has experienced in God's presence in the past:

> These things I remember
>   as I pour out my soul:
> how I would go with the throng
>   and lead them in procession to the house of God
> with glad shouts and songs of praise. (v. 4)

By faith, he also *looks ahead* to the day when the joy will be restored:

> Hope in God; for I shall again praise him,
> my salvation and my God. (vv. 5–6)

In the meantime, he determines to *look up*:

> My soul is downcast within me;
> therefore I remember you....
> By day the Lord commands his steadfast love,
> And at night his song is with me,
> a prayer to the God of my life. (vv. 6, 8)

The psalmist's pattern of honesty before God, remembrance of past joy, and persevering hope and faith can help get you through seasons of spiritual dryness. This may also be a time for thoughtful self-examination. Ask God to show you any specific issues that may be creating a barrier in your relationship with Him. Is there known sin that you've not confessed or repented of? Is there unforgiveness in your heart toward a family member or an individual who has wronged you? Is there some step of obedience you know God wants you to take that you have delayed? Some of the women I surveyed spoke of allowing anger or disappointment to put up walls in their relationship with God.

Dry spells can be evidence that we're in a rut in our devotional life. We may have become too focused on the mechanics we're going through rather than the meaning. Many times this can be dealt with by varying our routine. Recently when I felt the need for freshness in my devotional life, I took a few days out from my normal Bible reading schedule to review and meditate on some passages that I had memorized earlier.

Sometimes a period of dryness may simply be God's way of revealing what's in our heart—whether we love Him because of the sensations He gives us, or just because He is God.

Whatever the cause, those experiences are no reason to give up on meeting with God daily. My own experience, as well as the testimony of untold believers through the ages is that if we persevere through those dry spells, looking backward in remembrance and forward in hope, examining our hearts and seeking to grow, eventually the dry spell will give way to seasons of refreshment and joy.

"Truthfully, I don't have a strong desire to spend time with God."

- *What I need is a fresh touch from God to give me the desire to be in the Word more.*

We have all faced times when we just didn't have the hunger or desire to meet with the Lord. In the physical realm, when we're hungry we eat, at which point we're no longer hungry. The more we eat, the less hungry we are. In the spiritual world, however, just the opposite is true. The more we eat of spiritual food, the hungrier we become, and the more we want to eat.

The more you taste of the Word of God, the more you will long for it. The more you partake of Jesus, the Bread of Life, the more you'll hunger for Him. So if you don't have a craving for spiritual food, there's a good chance you've not been fueling those desires.

A closely related reason for lack of spiritual desire is that we may be filling ourselves with what the world has to offer, leaving us with little enthusiasm for spiritual food. When you tell your children they can't eat candy at five o'clock in the afternoon "because it will spoil your appetite," you realize that if they get filled with the quick rush sugar provides, they won't be hungry for the food you know they really need.

When the children of Israel moved from Egypt into the wilderness of Sinai, it took them a while to acquire a taste for manna, which seemed bland and boring compared to the spice and variety of the "onions, leeks, and garlic" they had enjoyed in Egypt. But God was interested in more than satisfying their taste buds; He knew what would really nourish and sustain them for the years in the wilderness. He wanted to wean them from the short-lived cheap thrills of Egypt so He could introduce them to the true joys of being fed by His hand and so He could cultivate in them a longing for the Promised Land.

If you're in the habit of feasting on what the world has to offer—books, podcasts, music, television, movies, social media, online shopping—you might find you have little appetite for the Word and prayer. So if you want to increase your hunger for the Lord, try weaning yourself from the world's diet.

Be prepared for some withdrawal symptoms when you put down your phone or cut back on activities you enjoy but that curb your hunger for the Lord. Don't worry—those feelings will go away. Then begin feeding on the Word of God.

At first, it may seem bland and boring, but in time you'll discover that it satisfies in a far deeper, richer way than those things you once thought were so filling.

"Sometimes God seems a million miles away."

- I seem to be having a daily monologue.

There are times when God withholds from us the conscious sense of His presence—times that God seems far away and we no longer have the feelings of intimacy we may once have enjoyed. I believe this is because He wants us to learn to walk by faith and to seek Him with all our hearts.

In the midst of extreme suffering, Job struggled to believe that God was there when he could not sense His presence.

> Behold, I go forward, but he is not there,
>   and backward, but I do not perceive him;
> on the left hand when he is working, I do not behold him;
>   he turns to the right hand, but I do not see him.
> (Job 23:8–9)

Then, with eyes of faith, Job declared what he knew to be true and affirmed his commitment to cling to the Lord and His Word in spite of what his feelings told him:

> But he knows the way that I take;
>   when he has tried me, I shall come out as gold....
> I have not departed from the commandment of his lips;
> I have treasured the words of his mouth more
>   than my portion of food. (Job 23:10, 12)

The Song of Solomon records two times when the young bride had a similar experience:

> On my bed by night
> I sought him whom my soul loves;
> I sought him, but found him not. (3:1)
>
> I opened to my beloved,
>   But my beloved had turned and gone. (5:6)

In both instances the painful (though only perceived)

absence caused the troubled bride to pursue her beloved earnestly until she found him. Her diligent search was rewarded with a restored consciousness of his presence as well as a renewed determination to stay close by his side.

Younger, less mature believers are often granted a special, conscious sense of God's presence. As we grow, however, He provides opportunities for us to trust Him even when we can't see Him. God is pleased with the faith that is strengthened in the darkness. That is what is at the heart of Isaiah's exhortation to those who have faithfully followed the Lord but cannot sense His presence:

> Who among you fears the LORD
> and obeys the voice of his servant?
> Let him who walks in darkness
> and has no light
> trust in the name of the LORD
> and rely on his God. (Isa. 50:10)

Don't Give Up!

The responses of the women I surveyed confirm that the enemy will throw these and other obstacles in our path to try to get us to live the Christian life apart from consistent, daily time in God's presence. At times you'll get discouraged and may feel like throwing in the towel. But don't do it.

Don't quit! Keep pursuing Him. Your search will be rewarded.

MAKE IT PERSONAL

1. Which of the obstacles discussed in this chapter do you most identify with? What suggestions would you make to a friend who was struggling with the same obstacles?

2. Think through your current schedule and identify any activities that may be hindering you from adequately prioritizing your relationship with the Lord.

3. What steps do you need to take to ensure that your relationship with the Lord is the most important priority in your life? Share those steps with a friend who will help hold you accountable.

4. Who do you know with a consistent devotional life? Ask one or more of those individuals to share with you how they've dealt with the specific obstacles you've encountered.

PART FIVE

The Practice of a Devotional Life

*I wait for the LORD ...
and in his word I hope.*

PS. 130:5

For over forty years now I have observed the Morning Watch. If God has used me in any way down through the years it is because I have met Him morning by morning. I solve my problems before I come to them. Without the Morning Watch my work would be ineffective. I would be weak and helpless. It is only when I wait upon Him that I become strong spiritually.

OSWALD J. SMITH

PART FIVE

SECTION ONE

Receiving His Word

Mary ... sat at Jesus' feet, and heard His word.
LUKE 10:39 NKJV

I saw that the most important thing I had to do was to give myself to the reading of the Word of God, and to meditation on it, that thus my heart might be comforted, encouraged, warned, reproved, instructed; and that thus, by means of the Word of God, whilst meditating on it, my heart might be brought into experimental communion with the Lord.

GEORGE MÜLLER

CHAPTER 7

The Wonder of the Word

"I must have a Bible of my own! I must have one, if I have to save up for it for ten years!"

The year was 1794. For as long as she could remember, little Mary Jones had yearned to hold a Bible in her hands so that she might read it for herself. For years she had sat at night on her weaver father's lap and listened to him tell the stories of Abraham, Joseph, David, and Daniel. But her family was far too poor to afford a Bible, even if one had been available, for Bibles could scarcely be found in all of Wales during those days.

Two years earlier, Mrs. Evans, the wife of a nearby farmer, had promised the child that when she learned to read, she could come to their house and read their Bible. So as soon as the first school opened in a neighboring village, Mary had eagerly set about learning to read.

Now, the ten-year-old girl had just walked two miles from

the North Wales village of Llanfihangel to the Evanses' farm. The distance was no object to the eager child: "I'd walk farther than that for such a pleasure, ma'am!" she'd said to Mrs. Evans.

Once Mary was finally left alone in the room with the Bible, she reverently lifted off the white napkin that covered and protected the cherished Book. Then, with trembling hands, she opened the Book to the fifth chapter of John, where her eyes lit on the words, "Search the Scriptures because you think that in them you have eternal life: and it is they that bear witness about me" (John 5:39). Confident that God had spoken to her directly, she earnestly vowed to search His Word with all her heart.

Every Saturday from that point on, Mary made the journey to the Evanses' farm, where she read, studied, and memorized entire chapters from the borrowed Bible. All the time, however, her heart ached, so great was her yearning to have a Bible of her own. She purposed that she must have a Bible at any cost.

For the next six years, in addition to continuing her school studies and the many chores to be tended to at home, Mary used every available moment to do odd jobs for friends and neighbors. Every penny she earned was carefully laid aside, until at long last she had saved enough to buy a Bible of her own.

When she learned that the closest place a Bible could be purchased was the town of Bala, some twenty-five miles away, there was no question in her mind about what she must do. With hope in her heart, she started out early one morning, walking barefoot so as not to ruin her one pair of shoes. Before she reached her destination, her feet were blistered and cut from the stones in the road.

Physically weary, but barely able to contain her excitement that her lifelong goal should be so nearly realized, Mary finally arrived in Bala, where she poured out her story to the minister, Mr. Thomas Charles. When she had finished, Mr. Charles reluctantly informed her that the last of the Bibles available for purchase had already been sold and that the handful of remaining Bibles had been promised to others. Furthermore, the Society that had printed the small quantity of Bibles in the Welsh language did not intend to print any more.

So great was Mary's disappointment that she began to sob uncontrollably. Touched by the intensity of her passion to have a Bible of her own, Mr. Charles decided that she must have one of the few Welsh Bibles left in his possession. Words cannot describe the ecstasy Mary felt as Mr. Charles placed into her hands the precious treasure for which she had prayed, wept, and hoarded all these years. Her heart sang as she walked the twenty-five miles back home, carrying her very own Bible, the Book that would remain her dearest friend and companion throughout her life.[1]

IF GOD HAD NEVER SPOKEN

Have you ever thought about what life would be like if God had never spoken? What if He had never communicated with human beings? What if He had never given us His written Word? Try to imagine a world in which no one had ever heard the voice of God, a world in which there was no Bible.

We would know He *exists*, because "the heavens declare the glory of God" (Ps. 19:1). But how would we know what He is like if we didn't have a Bible?

Had God not chosen to speak, to reveal Himself, we would

> Have you ever thought about what life would be like if God had never spoken? What if He had never communicated with human beings? What if He had never given us His written Word?

have no standard for right and wrong. We would not know how we are to live. We might experience some vague sense of guilt when we sinned, but we would not know why; nor would we know what to do about our sin. We would have no way of communicating with our Creator. Our lives would be pointless and frustrating.

Imagine having to go through life without knowing anything of the promises of God, the commands of God, the love and mercy of God, the will of God, or the ways of God.

Thankfully, we do not have to exist in such a spiritual vacuum. God *has* spoken. He *has* revealed Himself to human beings. Have you ever stopped to consider what that really means?

There are many natural wonders on our planet. And the human race has engineered, designed, and produced many scientific and technological marvels. But none come close to equaling the wonder of those three small words found in the first chapter of Genesis: *"And God said..."*

Think of it! The eternal God and Creator of the universe, the One who holds all the bodies of water on the earth in the palm of His hand, the One who uses the continents as His footstool, the One who measures the span of the universe with the width of His hand—that God has spoken to *us*, His finite but infinitely loved creatures.

In the spiritual realm, God has given us many marvelous gifts—divine wonders that make us stand in awe of His greatness, His power, and His love. The creation of the world, the Incarnation of the Lord Jesus, the miracle of the new birth—each of these marvels is inseparably linked to the *Word of God.*

When God *said,* "Let there be light," there *was* light. The "mere" spoken Word of God brought into being our entire universe. The apostle Peter reminds us that "by the word of God the heavens came into being long ago and the earth was brought about" (2 Peter 3:5 csb).

God's Word was active not only in creation, however, but also in the Incarnation. When the Lord of glory came to this earth as an infant in Bethlehem, *God* was speaking. "The Word became flesh and dwelt among us" (John 1:14).

It is that same Word, planted by the Spirit of God in our hearts, that causes us to be born again: "You have been born again, not of perishable seed but of imperishable, through the living and abiding word of God" (1 Peter 1:23).

Delighting in His Word

The older I get and the more I delve into the riches of God's Word, the more I find myself cherishing it, standing in awe of it, and delighting in it "like one who finds vast treasure" (Ps. 119:162 csb). I think this is what the psalmist must have felt as he contemplated the portion of God's Word that existed in his day. Throughout Psalm 119 King David seems hardly able to find adequate words to describe what he feels about the Word of God:

> Your testimonies are my delight;
> They are my counselors. (v. 24)

> O how I love your law!
>   It is my meditation all the day. (v. 97)
>
> How sweet are your words to my taste!
>   sweeter than honey to my mouth! (v. 103)
>
> I love your commandments
>   above gold, above fine gold. (v. 127)
>
> Your promise is well tried,
>   and your servant loves it. (v. 140)
>
> My heart stands in awe of your words. (v. 161)

David was not the only one to feel this way. No other book in history has received the acclaim and adulation given to the Bible. Listen to what some renowned men and women have been quoted as saying about the Bible:

> This great book . . . is the best book God has given to man. (US President Abraham Lincoln)

> The books of men have their day and grow obsolete. God's Word is like Himself, "the same yesterday, today, and forever." (nineteenth-century British cleric Robert Payne Smith)

> After more than sixty years of almost daily reading of the Bible, I never fail to find it always new and marvelously in tune with the changing needs of every day. (Hollywood director Cecil B. DeMille)

> To what greater inspiration and counsel can we turn than to the imperishable truth to be found in this treasure house, the Bible? (Queen Elizabeth II of England)

The highest earthly enjoyments are but a shadow of the joy I find in reading God's Word. (sixteenth-Century English noblewoman Lady Jane Grey)

The Bible is the greatest benefit which the human race has ever experienced.... A single line in the Bible has consoled me more than all the books I ever read beside. (German philosopher Immanuel Kant)

The Bible is God's chart for you to steer by, to keep you from the bottom of the sea, and to show you where the harbor is, and how to reach it without running on rocks and bars. (American preacher Henry Ward Beecher)

I hold one single sentence out of God's Word to be of more certainty and of more power than all the discoveries of all the learned men of all the ages. (British preacher Charles Spurgeon)

MORE PRECIOUS THAN GOLD

Even more important than what men and women think of the Word of God is what God says about His own Word. According to the Bible, the Word of the Lord is:

- true (Ps. 19:9; 33:4)
- pure (Ps. 12:6; 119:140 KJV; Prov. 30:5)
- righteous and fully trustworthy (Ps. 119:138 KJV)
- eternal and stands firm in the heavens (Ps. 119:89)
- divinely inspired (2 Tim. 3:16 NKJV; 2 Peter 1:21)
- profitable for our lives and walk (2 Tim. 3:16)
- perfect (Ps. 19:7)

- of greater value than any amount of gold or silver (Ps. 119:72)
- sweet to the taste (Ps. 19:9–10; 119:103; Ezek. 3:3).

The power and authority of God's Word infinitely surpass that of any other book that has ever been written. As a troubled young seminary professor, Martin Luther experienced the supernatural, transforming power of the Word, which later led him to write, "The Bible is alive, it speaks to me; it has feet, it runs after me; it has hands, it lays hold on me."[2]

When we pick up a copy of the Bible, do we fully realize what it is that we are holding in our hands? Do we ever stop to think that this is actually the *Word of God*? As Augustine reminds us, "When the Bible speaks, *God* speaks!"[3] But we in the West have been blessed with such easy access to the Word that it is hard not to take it for granted.

Margaret Nikol (1941–2020) remembered vividly what it was like not to have access to a Bible. It has been many years since I first heard Margaret share her testimony, but I've never forgotten her moving story.

A concert violinist, Margaret grew up in Bulgaria under one of Communism's most repressive regimes. Though her father was a pastor, even he did not own a Bible. The Communists had confiscated virtually all the Bibles in the country.

However, an elderly woman in Margaret's town managed to hold on to one Bible, which became a treasure shared—literally—by all the believers in the town. One by one, the pages were carefully torn from the Book and distributed. Margaret felt blessed to receive one page that included Genesis 16 and 17—a page she cherished and diligently studied. Her brother, who also became a pastor, had as his sole "library" a couple of pages from the Bible that he had copied by hand.

When Margaret was in her midthirties, she was exiled to the United States. Shortly after she arrived in America, some newfound friends asked what she would like for Christmas. Margaret didn't have to think long. More than anything else, she wanted a Bible.

Margaret described the day her friends took her to a Christian bookstore to make the purchase. It was the very first time she had ever seen a complete Bible: "There were red ones and black ones and green ones and blue ones and brown ones—every size, every shape—Bibles everywhere!" Overwhelmed by the sight, the thirty-seven-year-old woman stood in the aisle of that bookstore and "wept and wept and wept for joy!"

It is impossible for most of us to imagine what Margaret felt at that moment. Literally scores of Bibles line the shelves of my personal library—red, black, green, blue, and brown ones—every size—in at least a dozen different translations. That doesn't include a host of commentaries, concordances, reference books, devotional books, and hymnals.

Proverbs 27:7 tells us that

> One who is full loathes honey,
> but to one who is hungry everything bitter is sweet.

To hungry souls in parts of the world that have never been allowed to own a Bible, the Word of God is exceedingly sweet. But those of us who can hear the Word preached any hour of the day or night on our phones and laptops, in our houses and cars; who can walk into any bookstore and choose from an abundance of Bibles; and whose homes have multiple copies of the Bible, some of them unused—may find ourselves in danger of adopting a ho-hum attitude toward the Word of God.

If you've ever traveled in the Middle East, you may have observed the utmost reverence that Muslims show to their holy book, the Qur'an. You will never see them placing a copy of the Qur'an on the floor or treating it casually. Rather, the Qur'an is to be kept above the level of their heads and above all other books in the room. They treat their holy book with great care, keeping it wrapped in a special cloth and placing it on a special stand when they wish to read it. They believe that every word in the book is holy and that it should be highly respected. Doesn't the holy Word of God deserve at least the same respect—if not much more?

The Scripture says that God has exalted His Word above even His own name (Ps. 138:2 NKJV). If God esteems His Word that highly, what should be our attitude toward the Word? God says through the prophet Isaiah,

> I will look favorably on this kind of person:
> one who is humble, submissive in spirit,
> and *trembles* at my word. (Isa. 66:2; see also Ps. 119:161)

To tremble at the Word of the Lord means to have an attitude of reverential awe and fear. My dad had a great reverence and love for the Word of God. As a way of demonstrating that respect, he made it a habit never to place anything on top of the Bible. I've adopted this practice myself, not because the pulp and leather have any mystical properties or inherent value, but as a practical, visible means of honoring what is contained in those pages.

THE WONDER OF THE WORD

OUR MOST VALUABLE TREASURE

In Psalm 119, David can scarcely contain his joy as he rehearses the many blessings and benefits to be found in God's Word. It has power to keep us from sin (vv. 9, 11), to strengthen us when we are grieving (v. 28), to comfort us when we are suffering (vv. 50, 52), to grant us freedom (v. 45), to give us understanding and light for our path (v. 104), and to give us peace and keep us from stumbling (v. 165).

The Word of God will light your way. It will help you make right choices. It will heal your wounds and settle your heart, warn you of danger, protect and cleanse you from sin, lead you and make you wise. It is bread; it is water; it is a counselor; it is life. It is satisfying. It is sufficient. It is supreme. It is supernatural.

> *The Word of God will light your way. It will help you make right choices. It will heal your wounds and settle your heart, warn you of danger, protect and cleanse you from sin, lead you and make you wise.*

When I was a child in Christian school, we sometimes sang a hymn written in 1803 that reflects on the "precious treasure" that is ours in this Book:

> Holy Bible, Book divine,
>   Precious treasure, thou art mine:
> Mine to tell me whence I came;
>   Mine to teach me what I am.
>
> Mine to chide me when I rove,
>   Mine to show a Savior's love;
> Mine thou art to guide and guard;
>   Mine to punish or reward.

> Mine to comfort in distress,
>   Suff'ring in this wilderness;
> Mine to show, by living faith,
>   We can triumph over death.
>
> Mine to tell of joys to come,
>   And the rebel sinner's doom:
> O thou Holy Book divine,
>   Precious treasure, thou art mine.[4]

PREPARING TO MEET GOD IN HIS WORD

Preparation is something we're familiar with in lots of areas of life.

If you know you have an important meeting with your boss and the owner of the company first thing tomorrow morning, when do you begin preparing for it? Do you wait until after you get up in the morning—until you've exercised, showered, dressed, and eaten—before you start thinking about getting ready for your meeting? Do you all of a sudden look at your watch, realize the meeting has already begun, grab some crumpled clothes out of the dirty laundry and throw them on as you race to the car, arrive thirty minutes late to the meeting, sit down at the table where the others are already assembled, and then hastily start scribbling out notes for your presentation? Not if you care about your job.

When you announce to your kids that the family is going to take a trip to visit their favorite cousins when school gets out in two weeks, do they forget about it until it's time to get in the car to leave? If your children are like the ones I know, they have their suitcases packed a week ahead of time! They plan all the fun things they're going to do together. You can hardly get them to think about anything else.

While taking cello lessons as a teen, I learned that I couldn't just pick up the instrument and begin to play—not if I wanted to make beautiful music. First, I had to go through a series of steps. The bow needed to be tightened and lubricated with resin. The height of the cello had to be adjusted correctly. Each string had to be tuned. All these preparations directly affected the outcome of my playing.

When I host gatherings in our home, I make preparations. Lots of them. I have lists of my lists and sometimes spent the better part of days getting ready for the guests to arrive.

Whether it's for critical meeting, a family vacation, making music, or hosting guests, preparation matters. And preparation is no less crucial to meeting with God and cultivating a relationship with Him through His Word.

I have found that one of the greatest hindrances to a meaningful quiet time is the failure to prepare. Hour after hour throughout each day, our eyes and ears are lured by the world around us. The sights, sounds, and demands of our surroundings have a way of capturing our attention. That's why we often find ourselves distracted, hurried, and having quiet times with minds and hearts that are far from quiet. A little bit of preparation can make a big difference.

Some Practical Steps

As much as possible, I try to prepare for my morning time in the Word the night before, so my mind can be free to concentrate on the Lord in the morning. I'm not naturally an organized person, but I have found that disciplining myself to plan ahead can greatly enhance the quality of the time I spend alone with the Lord.

For example, I've found it helps to keep my Bible, journal, pen, devotional books, and other tools (more about those in chapter 9) together in the place where I plan to meet with the Lord in the morning. If I have to run around gathering those items, valuable time is lost, and my mind is distracted before I even begin.

As we pointed out in the last chapter, another key to success in meeting God in the morning is to get to bed early enough the night before. It's tough to stay up all hours of the night and then be alert and attentive to the Lord first thing in the morning. Getting to bed at a reasonable hour may require putting the children to bed earlier, making fewer evening commitments, getting chores done earlier in the evening, or turning off the TV and closing laptops and devices. Speaking of which . . .

If the last thing on our minds at night is the raucous sound of late-night entertainment on television or a zillion images and reels we've just scrolled through on our phone, we're not likely to waken the next morning prepared and eager to seek the Lord. As an alternative, why not try playing worship songs as the family is preparing for bed? Maintaining a calm, worshipful atmosphere at home in the evening may also help children sleep more peacefully at night and have a more settled spirit in the morning.

Lie Down in Peace

Devoting our final waking moments to meditating on the Lord and His Word helps to prepare for meeting with Him in the morning. Psalm 4, which may well be a prayer that David prayed before he went to sleep at night, offers us a model for this practice. Notice that even though he is in the midst of stressful circumstances, there's no panic in his tone. His spirit is serene as he directs his thoughts heavenward:

> Ponder in your hearts on your beds and be silent. . . .
> Offer right sacrifices
>   and put your trust in the Lord. . . .
> There are many who say, "Who will show us some good?
>   Lift up the light of your face upon us, O Lord!"
> You have put more joy in my heart
>   than they have when their grain and wine abound.
> In peace I will both lie down and sleep,
>   for you alone, O Lord, make me dwell in safety.
> (vv. 4–8)

There are other prayers in the psalms that I can imagine David voicing to the Lord just before his eyes closed in sleep at night:

> How precious to me are your thoughts, O God!
>   How vast is the sum of them!
> If I would count them, they are more than the sand.
>   I awake, and I am still with you. (Ps. 139:17–18)

> As for me, I shall behold your face in righteousness;
>   when I awake, I shall be satisfied with your likeness.
> (Ps. 17:15)

Before falling asleep at night, you may want to pray something like this: "Father, by Your Spirit, please minister to my spirit through the night. As I sleep, fill my subconscious mind with thoughts of Jesus. And may I awake beholding His likeness—thinking of and loving Him, satisfied with You and prepared to seek Your face."

"When I Awake..."

At the first sound of the alarm going off in the morning, we're faced with a choice. (That's assuming the choice was made the night before to set the alarm early enough to allow for unhurried time with the Lord before diving into the rest of the day's business.)

What we do in those first moments of wakefulness will either help or hinder us in cultivating intimacy with God through time in His Word.

You may be one of those people whose first response to the sound of the alarm is to push the "reality delayer" (aka snooze button). Somehow, at that moment, a few more minutes of sleep may seem a lot more appealing than digging into the Word.

Or if you're like me, as soon as your eyes open, you begin to think about all the things you have to do that day. As soon as you're on your feet, you're immediately tempted to begin attending to unfinished tasks around the house. (This is something I battle regularly, as my office is in my home and the to-do piles never seem to go away!)

Puritan pastor Lewis Bayly encouraged a different choice and explained why it's important to turn the heart to the Lord before doing anything else in the morning:

> As soon as ever thou awakest in the morning, keep the door of thy heart fast shut, that no earthly thought may enter, before that God come in first; and let him, before all others, have the first place there. So all evil thoughts either will not dare to come in, or shall the easier be kept out; and the heart will more savour of piety and godliness all the day after; but if thy heart be not, at thy first waking,

filled with some meditations of God and His word, ... Satan will attempt to fill it with worldly cares or fleshly desires, so that it will grow unfit for the service of God all the day after....

Begin, therefore, every day's work with God's word and prayer ... and as soon as thou awakest say to Him thus:

My soul waiteth on Thee, O Lord, more than the morning watch watcheth for the morning! O God, therefore be merciful unto me, and bless me, and cause thy face to shine upon me! Fill me with thy mercy this morning, so shall I rejoice and be glad all my days.[5]

TUNING THE HEART

What Bayly was suggesting is that our hearts need to be "tuned" to the Lord, much as a musical instrument needs to be tuned to an absolute pitch before it can make beautiful music. Over the years I've used various means to get my heart in tune with His so that my time in the Word will be fruitful.

At times, the words of Isaiah 50:4–5 have helped tune my heart. Even before getting out of bed in the morning, I will sometimes meditate on this passage and pray it back to the Lord—something like this:

> The Sovereign LORD has given me an instructed tongue,
> to know the word that sustains the weary.

Lord God, You are my Lord. You are the sovereign God. I want You to reign in my life this day. I know that today You will bring people into my life—family members, friends, fellow workers, people I don't even know, people who are weary and need a word from You to sustain and encourage them. I will not know how to speak the words they need to hear unless You first instruct me.

> He wakens me morning by morning,
>   wakens my ear to listen like one being taught.

Thank You, Lord, for waking me this morning. Before I can teach others, I must be taught by You. Before I open my mouth to speak to others, I need to listen to You. Please open my ears to hear what You want to say to me this day.

> The Sovereign LORD has opened my ears,
>   and I have not been rebellious;
> I have not drawn back.

As You speak to me, may my heart be submissive toward You. May I not resist anything that You say to me today.

Sometimes I'll read a selection from a devotional book as a means of tuning my heart before I open Scripture. These books, written by human authors, should never take the place of the Word of God itself, but they help us focus on spiritual matters and clear out any clutter that may be distracting us. (In the appendix you'll find a list of some of the devotional books that have been a blessing to me over the years.)

Hymns that express a longing and a desire to hear the voice of God can be another means of getting our hearts in tune. Here are two classic hymns I have often sung or read as my prayer to the Lord:

> Speak, Lord, in the stillness
>   While I wait on Thee;
> Hushed my heart to listen,
>   In expectancy.

Speak, O blessed Master,
   In this quiet hour,
Let me see Thy face, Lord,
   Feel Thy touch of power.

For the words Thou speakest,
   "They are life" indeed;
Living Bread from heaven,
   Now my spirit feed![6]

* * *

Open my eyes, that I may see
   Glimpses of truth Thou hast for me;
Place in my hands the wonderful key,
   That shall unclasp and set me free.
Silently now I wait for Thee,
   Ready, my God, Thy will to see;
Open my eyes, illumine me,
   Spirit divine![7]

Now, with hearts tuned and spiritual ears and eyes attentive to Him, we open the pages of that wondrous Book, expecting to encounter its Author and to be transformed in His presence.

MAKE IT PERSONAL

1. Plan a time into your schedule when you can read through Psalm 119 aloud in one sitting. You may want to do this alone or as a family or with a group of friends. The psalm is divided into twenty-two eight-verse stanzas. If you're with others, take turns reading the stanzas until you've read through the entire Psalm.

2. Now look back over Psalm 119 and make a list of the characteristics of God's Word and the benefits and blessings it is intended to bring to our lives.

3. Write a prayer thanking the Lord for His Word and for what it has meant in your life.

4. Record two or three practical steps you could take to better prepare your heart to receive the Word each day.

CHAPTER 8

Getting into the Word

No doubt you've heard people say that they just can't understand the Bible or that they don't get anything out of it. In my experience, one of the biggest reasons the Bible remains a mystery to people is simply that they don't read it! With tongue in cheek, one writer suggested that "if all the neglected Bibles were dusted simultaneously, we would have a record dust storm and the sun would go into eclipse for a whole week!"[1]

God promises a blessing to those who read His Word (Rev. 1:3). At the beginning of their reigns, the kings of Israel were commanded to write out by hand a copy of the law of God; then they were to read that copy every day for the rest of their lives so they would learn to fear the Lord and keep His commandments (Deut. 17:18–20). Later, through His prophet Isaiah, God commanded the Israelites to "seek and read from the book of the Lord" (Isa. 34:16). On more than one occasion in the Old Testament, revival broke out when God's people began to read His Word after a time of neglect (Neh. 8–10; 2 Chron. 34:14–33).

The Gospels record several instances where Jesus turned to His critics and said, in effect, "Haven't you read . . . ?" (Matt. 12:3; 12:55; 19:4; 21:16; 21:42). He expected them to have already read and applied the Scripture before questioning Him, and when they needed to be corrected, He sent them back to the Word of God.

This focus on reading and learning from Scripture continued into the early days of the church. Acts 8:27–39 tells of an Ethiopian official whose life was changed while reading a scroll of the book of Isaiah. With a little guidance from the apostle Philip, the official's eyes were opened, and God gave his heart repentance, faith, and salvation (Acts 8:27–39).

When the apostle Paul sent his divinely inspired letter to the church at Colossae, he wanted to be sure the believers there not only shared this letter this among themselves, but also read and shared the one he had sent to the believers in Laodicea (Col. 4:16). Similarly, he wrote to the Thessalonians, "I put you under oath before the Lord to have this letter read to all the brothers" (1 Thess. 5:27). And Paul exhorted the young pastor Timothy to make the public reading of Scripture a high priority (1 Tim. 4:13).

Oswald Chambers emphasized the importance of reading the Scripture:

> The mere reading of the Word of God has power to communicate the life of God to us mentally, morally and spiritually. God makes the words of the Bible a sacrament, i.e., the means whereby we partake of His life; it is one of His secret doors for the communication of His life to us.[2]

READ PRAYERFULLY

Simply reading Scripture on a regular basis is an obvious and vital starting place for getting into the Word. But the way we approach the text matters. We must not only read, but also read prayerfully. Ask God to give you understanding. Ask Him to open up to you those portions that are difficult to grasp. Ask Him to make familiar passages fresh and alive to your heart. Ask Him to reveal Himself, His heart, and His ways to you through the reading of His Word.

Puritan pastor William Gurnall (1616–1679) wrote eloquently of the need to read the Scripture prayerfully:

> Go to God by prayer for a key to unlock the mysteries of His word. It is not the plodding but the praying soul, that will get this treasure of scripture knowledge. God often brings a truth to the Christian's hand as a return of prayer, which he had long hunted for in vain with much labour and study: "There is a God in heaven that revealeth secrets" (Dan. 2:28); and where doth He reveal the secrets of His word but at the throne of grace?[3]

A practice that has resulted in great blessing has been to begin my time in the Word by praying Scriptures such as these back to the Lord:

> Open my eyes that I may behold
>   wondrous things out of your law....
> Give me understanding, that I may keep your law
>   and observe it with my whole heart....
>
> Make me to know your ways, O Lord,
>   teach me your paths;
> Lead me in your truth and teach me,

> for you are God of my salvation;
> for you I wait all the day long....
>
> Teach me what I do not see;
> if I have done iniquity, I will do it no more.
> (Ps. 119:18, 34; 25:4–5; Job 34:32)

As I pray those words, I am expressing two things to the Lord. First, I am acknowledging that this is not an ordinary book I am about to read, but a *supernatural one,* and that, therefore, I need the assistance of its Author. We need the Holy Spirit, who inspired this book, to give us wisdom and understanding, to be our teacher, and to shed divine light on the Word.

The Bible itself reminds us of this truth. First Corinthians 2:14 tells us that "human wisdom" cannot understand the things of God—that only the Spirit of God can open them up to us. And James 1:5 advises, "If any of you lacks wisdom, let him ask God, who gives generously to all without reproach, and it will be given him."

The second thing I express with my morning prayer—and this is so important—is a promise. When I pray, "Give me understanding," I also commit to obey whatever God says to me through His Word:

> ...that I may keep your law
> and observe it with my whole heart. (Ps. 119:34)

Or, in other words: "Please speak to me. And whether I like it or not, whether I agree with it or not, whether it is easy or not, by Your enabling grace and power, *I will do what You say.*"

Frances Ridley Havergal, the beloved nineteenth-century hymn writer, beautifully expressed this commitment to obey:

> Master, speak! and make me ready,
> When Thy voice is truly heard,
> With obedience glad and steady
> Still to follow every word.[4]

READ THOUGHTFULLY

When my siblings and I were teens, our dad encouraged us to take a course in speed-reading. However, he suggested that there were two things that should never be speed-read: love letters and the Bible.

Most of us wouldn't think of hastily skimming through a love letter. Rather, we pore over its words and read and reread them, searching for every nuance of meaning we can possibly glean from between the lines. Should we approach the Bible any less carefully? After all, it is also a "love letter"— it reveals God's heart to us. And the more thoughtfully we read it, the more we will grasp His loving heart and intentions toward us.

Those who read the Bible hastily or casually will never mine its riches and plumb its depths for themselves. Psalm 19:10 tells us that the Word of God is

> *Those who read the Bible hastily or casually will never mine its riches and plumb its depths for themselves.*

> more to be desired ... than gold,
> even much fine gold.

You don't walk down the street and just stumble onto vast stores of gold. Gold is a precious, rare commodity that is buried deep in the earth. Significant time and effort are required to search for it and extract it from the rock in which it is embedded.

During his forty-year reign as the king of Israel, Solomon sent envoys far and wide throughout the earth in search of priceless earthly treasures. But he also understood the importance of searching earnestly for the wealth of God's ways. That is why he wrote to his son:

> If you call out for insight
>   and raise your voice for understanding,
> if you seek it like silver
>   and search for it as for hidden treasures,
> then you will understand the fear of the LORD
>   and find the knowledge of God. (Prov. 2:3–5)

Solomon's advice applies to us as well. As you read the Bible, take care to meditate on the meaning of what you are reading. Absorb the Word into your system by dwelling on it, pondering it, going over it again and again in your mind, considering it from many different angles. Spend time with it until it becomes a part of *you*. Be ever mining it for treasure.

The English Puritan preacher and author Thomas Watson wrote both eloquently and practically of this process:

> Without meditation the truths which we know will never affect our hearts.... As an hammer drives a nail to the head, so meditation drives a truth to the heart.... Read before you meditate. "Give attendance to reading" (1 Tim. iv:13). Then it follows, "meditate upon these things" (v. 15). Reading doth furnish with matter; it is the oil that feeds the lamp of meditation. Be sure your meditations are founded upon Scripture. Reading without meditation is unfruitful; meditation without reading is dangerous.[5]

One of the most valuable aids to meditation is Scripture memorization. In fact, when I encounter someone who is battling discouragement or depression, I often ask two questions: "Are you singing to the Lord?" and "Are you memorizing Scripture?" These two exercises are not some magical formula to make all our problems go away, but they do have incredible power to change our perspective and attitude toward the issues we are facing.

"But I just can't memorize," some will quickly respond. In his excellent book on spiritual disciplines, Donald Whitney points out that the issue is more likely to be motivation, not ability:

> What if I offered you one thousand dollars for every verse you could memorize in the next seven days? Do you think your attitude toward Scripture memory and your ability to memorize would improve? Any financial reward would be minimal when compared to the accumulating value of the treasure of God's Word deposited within your mind.[6]

The fact is, we can and do memorize all the time. We memorize people's names, directions to places we frequent, credit card numbers, and phone numbers. How? We remember information that is important to us or that we often use or repeat. Scripture memorization is no different. It requires motivation and regular, systematic review.

If you've not memorized Scripture before, I suggest starting with small portions, perhaps one or two verses a week. Select verses that relate to specific concerns or needs in your life. You may want to write or print them out on a card that you can keep with you and review several times a day—or even record them in an app on your phone. I've found that reviewing these verses while going to sleep at night, when I waken during the night, and when I first wake up in the morning, helps reinforce them in my memory.

Once you've mastered a verse or a paragraph, go on to the next, while continuing to review the verses you've memorized most recently. You may find it helpful to memorize with a partner so you can encourage each other and recite Scripture to each other.

Scripture memory and meditation will bring about many benefits in your life, including

- *cleansing and renewing your mind*
- *keeping you from sin*
- *providing insight and direction in the midst of real-life situations*
- *strengthening your spirit*
- *combating the attacks of the enemy on your mind and emotions*
- *stimulating spiritual desires*
- *diminishing the demands of your flesh*
- *protecting you from wrong thinking patterns*
- *fixing your mind and affections on "things above" (Col. 3:2)*
- *creating a stored-up treasury of spiritual resources for the future*

Darlene Deibler Rose (1917–2004) provided dramatic evidence of this last benefit in her moving autobiographical book, *Evidence Not Seen*. As a young American missionary, Rose spent four years in a Japanese prison camp during World War II. In her book she recalls the way God used Scriptures she had memorized as a child to sustain her through her terrifying ordeal:

As a child and young person, I had had a driving compulsion to memorize the written Word. In the cell I was grateful now for those days in Vacation Bible School, when I had memorized many single verses, complete chapters, and Psalms, as well as whole books of the Bible. In the years that followed, I reviewed the Scriptures often. The Lord fed me with the Living Bread that had been stored against the day when fresh supply was cut off by the loss of my Bible. He brought daily comfort and encouragement—yes, and joy—to my heart through the knowledge of the Word.... I had never needed the Scriptures more than in these months on death row, but since so much of His Word was there in my heart, it was not the punishment the Kempeitai had anticipated when they took my Bible.[7]

READ SYSTEMATICALLY

Imagine that you get hungry while reading this book, so you decide to took a break and make yourself a sandwich. What would happen if you just open the refrigerator, close your eyes, and grab whatever items your hand happens to reach first? Instead of a peanut butter and jelly sandwich, you might end up with a plate of onions, mustard, and whipped cream. Not especially appetizing or nourishing, right?

That's a picture of the way many people approach the Word of God. They blindly "grab" whatever passage they come to first, in no particular sequence or order. When passages are separated from their context like that, their meaning can be changed, and well-meaning believers can easily misunderstand what they read.

Others read the Bible much like a teenager whose preferred

> Our bodies require a nutritionally balanced diet in order to stay healthy. Likewise, our spirits need the balance that comes from taking in the "whole counsel of God," not limiting ourselves to those passages that seem particularly appetizing.

diet consists of pizza, chips, soft drinks, and ice cream. Our bodies require a nutritionally balanced diet in order to stay healthy. Likewise, our spirits need the balance that comes from taking in the "whole counsel of God," not limiting ourselves to those passages that seem particularly appetizing. The spiritual growth of some believers has been stunted due to a scriptural "diet" that consists primarily of the Psalms with perhaps a smidgen of the New Testament Epistles.

It's true that not all parts of the Bible are equally appetizing or easy to digest. When I come to portions of 1 Chronicles and Ezekiel in my Bible reading, I have to admit that some of those passages seem tedious or even unnecessary, especially as compared to the more "succulent" passages I've read in 1 Peter or the Gospel of John. Even the great Puritan pastor and author John Bunyan admitted, "I have sometimes seen more in a line of the Bible than I could well tell how to stand under, and yet at another time the whole Bible hath been to me as dry as a stick."[8]

But Paul reminded Timothy that "*all* Scripture is breathed out by God and profitable for teaching, for reproof, for correction, and for training in righteousness" (2 Tim. 3:16). That means that a balanced scriptural intake needs to include *all* of God's Word.

One reason we may resist this is that we have become so accustomed to having our senses stimulated by visual and audible thrills that we are easily bored by anything that does not yield immediate excitement and rewards. But as Oswald Chambers wisely pointed out, "the Bible does not thrill, the Bible nourishes. Give time to the reading of the Bible and the recreating effect is as real as that of fresh air physically."[9]

The eighteenth-century British pastor Richard Cecil put it this way:

> The Bible resembles an extensive and highly cultivated garden, where there is a vast variety and profusion of fruits and flowers, some of which are more essential or more splendid than others; but there is not a blade suffered to grow in it which has not its use and beauty in the system.[10]

Yes, we need the Psalms and the Epistles. But we also need the Books of the Law, the Historical Books, the Prophets, and the Gospels. We need the whole of God's Word. And we need to read it in such a way that we get a sense of its flow—how the various parts of the Bible fit together and the parts fit into the whole.

When we pick up an ordinary book, we don't generally start in the middle and jump around haphazardly from chapter to chapter—especially if the book has a plot. But that is the way many of us read the Word of God. We have failed to see that the Bible has a plot, too, that it is one grand story that has a beginning and a conclusion. It is the story of redemption—the story of a God who created human beings for fellowship with Himself, watched as they rejected His overtures again and again, and then stooped down to restore men and women to intimacy with Himself through the cross.

The fact that the Bible is a whole doesn't mean it can

only be read straight through from Genesis to Revelation, although I have experienced great blessing in doing this on a regular basis. It does mean that context and flow are important. Individual verses need to be read in the context of the paragraph and chapter in which they appear. Chapters should be studied in light of the entire book where they are found. And the various books make more sense if we understand how they fit into the scheme and flow of the Bible as a whole and of God's eternal, redemptive plan.

If you want to get a balanced spiritual diet as well as an understanding of the whole plan of God, make sure that you are not overlooking or bypassing certain portions of the Word.

Different Approaches

There are many different, systematic Bible reading plans available online,[11] some designed to help you read through the entire Bible in a year, others in a longer time span. I have used a number of these over the years.

One approach I particularly appreciate is to read in both the Old and New Testaments at the same time—for several reasons. First, the Old Testament sheds light on the New and vice versa. Those connections are easier to see when I am reading in both Testaments. Second, I don't like to go for long periods of time without reading in the Gospels, where we get the clearest picture of Jesus. If the goal of our devotional life is to know Him and to be conformed to His image, then we will want to go back to the Gospels over and over again. Third, reading in both Testaments usually balances the more difficult Old Testament passages with other portions that are easier to "digest."

My father had an approach to Bible reading that he rarely varied. Each morning he read five chapters from the Psalms and one from the Proverbs, thus reading through the Psalms and Proverbs every month. Then he read two chapters consecutively from the Old Testament and one from the New.

Many years ago, a dear, older pastor (now in heaven) recommended a Bible reading plan that I have found to be a great blessing. He suggested dividing the Bible into six major sections beginning in Genesis, Joshua, Job, Isaiah, Matthew, and Romans; reading one or more chapters consecutively in each of those sections daily; then simply bookmarking the end of the day's reading in each section, making it easy to simply pick up the next day.

This has been one of my favorite ways to read the Word because it highlights the flow of the biblical story. Though penned by many different authors over a period of fifteen hundred years, it displays a unity and coherence that can only be supernatural. When I have followed this system, I have often found that what I was reading in one portion dovetailed precisely with what I was reading in another.

At times you may feel the need to take a particular book or section of the Bible and "place it under a microscope." One way of doing that is to choose a shorter book and read through it every day for thirty days. This is a good way to gain deeper insight into the heart and message of an individual book.

You will probably find that your devotional life stays fresher if you vary your approach to Bible reading periodically. At times you may want to read just a small portion each day, meditating on each word and phrase (the microscope approach). During other seasons you may want to cover more ground more quickly, looking for the broader, overarching themes. Occasionally you may wish to take a break from reading consecutively in order to focus on a particular topic, word, or character from the Bible. However, I'd encourage you not to neglect systematic reading of the Scripture for extended periods of time.

On occasion, I have found great value in reading through the Scripture at a more rapid pace than normal, in order to get a panoramic, bird's-eye view of God's plan. And what a magnificent view that is.

Certain themes run like rivers from Genesis to Revelation. To use another metaphor, those themes weave together like threads in a great tapestry to tell the story of redemption. God's plan to create and redeem a race for Himself; His unending love, mercy, and grace; His long-suffering toward sinners, and yet His righteous judgment against those who refuse to repent; Satan's wiles and his persistent, relentless hatred of and rebellion against God; Satan's never-ending attempts to persuade humanity to join him in his sedition; God's ultimate, decisive triumph over Satan and His eternal rule over heaven and earth and hell—these are some of the strands that have unfolded before me as I've looked at Scripture as a whole.

Reading the Bible in this way has given me greater understanding and appreciation of the ways of God. For example, as I have walked with both Old and New Testament saints, I have seen that faith pleases God. Through those seemingly endless Old Testament laws and instructions concerning the offering of sacrifices, I've been reminded that sin is costly and that only a blood sacrifice can atone for it. As I've moved from the old to the new covenant, I've heard the sweet music of the gospel—the glad refrain that the blood of Jesus, the spotless Lamb of God, satisfies the wrath of God against sin and cleanses the sinner's guilty conscience.

On virtually every page from Genesis to Revelation, I have seen the likeness and the signature of the Lord Jesus. I have marveled and wondered and wept at the glory of His presence, at His redeeming love, at the spectacle of the cross, and at the hope that is ours through Him.

DON'T GET DISCOURAGED!

As meaningful as my time in Scripture has been to me, I want to be quick to say that not every day or every portion has been a spiritual feast, any more than every meal I eat is a mouthwatering feast. In all honesty, some passages have tasted more like cardboard than honey! Some days I have felt like I was trudging through mud rather than "Walking in the King's Highway."[12] (Even the apostle Peter acknowledged that some of Paul's writings were "hard to understand"— 2 Peter 3:16.)

However, the value and impact of the Word in our lives cannot necessarily be seen in one day's or one week's intake. When your kids are growing up, you don't usually see evidence of physical growth on a daily basis. But gradually you realize that their pants are getting shorter and their arms are protruding from their sleeves. At the end of the year, when they stand up against the wall where you measure height, you're amazed to realize how much they've grown.

Likewise, the value of a balanced, nutritious diet is not generally experienced in one day or one week. Rather, the cumulative benefits of eating right—or the consequences of not eating right—are experienced over an extended period of time.

Our spiritual growth from the Word works much the

same way. We usually don't see a lot of change overnight. But when we stop and look back over a period of months or years, we realize the extent to which the study of Scripture has shaped and molded our lives. The consequences of a poor spiritual diet may not be immediately apparent, either, but they definitely will be evident in the long run.

So don't give up when you come across portions of Scripture that seem to make no sense or have no apparent value. And don't conclude that those portions are worthless. Oswald Chambers exhorts, "*Read* the Bible, whether you understand it or not, and the Holy Spirit will bring back some word of Jesus to you in a particular set of circumstances and make it living."[13]

Remember that whether we understand it or not, whether it is easy reading or not, the Word of God—all of it—is still profitable (2 Tim. 3:16). Unlike any other book that has ever been written, the Bible is alive, and it comes with a personal tutor—the Holy Spirit who lives in us. His job is to teach us what we need to know and to give us understanding of spiritual truth that we cannot perceive with our natural minds.

Even those passages that are most difficult to grasp or that seem to be of relatively little value have a sanctifying effect on our spirits. As Jesus said to His disciples, "Already you are clean because of the word that I have spoken to you" (John 15:3). Often after I have finished reading a portion for the day, I will pray and ask the Lord to cleanse my spirit, my heart, my mind, and my life with the water of His Word (Eph. 5:26).

DON'T FORGET THE GOAL!

Whatever approach you take to reading the Bible, don't let yourself become a slave to the method. Don't get so caught up in the mechanics that you miss the point.

Remember that the goal is not how fast—or how slowly—you get through the Bible. The goal is to get the Word into your heart and life and to cultivate an intimate relationship with Jesus. It's possible to "know" this Book academically from cover to cover while failing to see and know Jesus, the living Word of God.

One of the most sobering passages in the Bible has to do with this concern. The Pharisees of Jesus' day were renowned for their vast, superior knowledge of the Old Testament Scriptures. Yet one day Jesus looked them squarely in the eye and said, "You have never heard [the Father's] voice, his form you have never seen, and you do not have his word abiding in you" (John 5:37–38).

I can just see those indignant Bible scholars turning red in the face and sputtering under their breath: "What does he mean? Who does he think he is? He's just a blue-collar worker! He's never even been to seminary! And *he's* telling *us* that we have never heard God speak and that His Word doesn't dwell in us? Why, we've spent our whole lives mastering the Scriptures! If *we* haven't heard God's voice, who has?"

But Jesus wasn't finished. He went on: "You search the Scriptures because you think that in them you have eternal life; and it is they that bear witness about *me*, yet you refuse to come to *me* that you might have life" (John 5:39–40).

What was Jesus saying? He wanted those men to understand that they had missed the whole point of studying Scripture. The purpose of getting into the Word of God is to

> Remember that the goal is not how fast—or how slowly—you get through the Bible. The goal is to get the Word into your heart and life and to cultivate an intimate relationship with Jesus.

meet Jesus. *He* is the object of our pursuit; He *is* the Word! It's all about *Him*. If we master the Bible but don't end up knowing, loving, worshiping, serving, and being like Jesus, we are really no better than the devil himself.

PRESS ON TO THE TOP

One of my favorite vacation spots is in western Wyoming, near the Grand Teton mountain range. Years ago I had the privilege of staying in a home that faces those majestic peaks. Early one morning I left the house for a mountain walk. But fog had settled in over the area and the entire range seemed to have disappeared.

Even though the view was much less than spectacular, I began what for me was a moderately difficult climb up the mountain. Soon my heart was beating faster. I began to perspire, and my legs felt wooden. I was not doing this for fun—my idea of fun is more along the lines of doing jigsaw puzzles; I certainly was not doing it for the view—the mountains were shrouded in fog. I pressed on that day only because I knew the exercise was good for me.

Then it happened. All of a sudden my ascent took me above the fog, and my efforts were rewarded with an incredible view of the towering Tetons. It was as if those magnificent, snow-covered mountains peaks just burst forth out of the earth. For a moment I forgot my racing pulse and tired legs. The view at the top made all that effort worth it.

Proverbs 25:2 says,

> It is the glory of God to conceal things,
>   but the glory of kings is to search things out.

The fact that there are some things—many things!—that God knows but we don't is what makes Him God and us human. An essential part of God's glory and splendor is that He cannot be fully known by finite creatures. At the same time, *our* glory is to devote ourselves to searching out His ways, believing that one day our search will be rewarded.

Paul puts it another way. He reminds us that "now we see in a mirror dimly" and "know in part." In other words, we know there is a stunning view out there, but from our current vantage point we can't see it; it is obscured by the fog of time and space. But Paul goes on to give us reason for great hope and anticipation: "*Then* [we shall see] face to face. . . . Then I shall know fully, even as I am fully known" (1 Cor. 13:12).

Yes, the pathway may be steep; hiking through Leviticus, 1 Chronicles, and Revelation may seem strenuous and leave us with aching spiritual muscles. But for those who press on to know Him, we have God's promise that one day we will step out of the fog into brilliant, clear, dazzling sunlight. The view at the top will be spectacular, for that is where at long last we "will see his face" (Rev. 22:4)—Jesus Himself, in all of His glory. And that's one view that will be well worth the wait!

MAKE IT PERSONAL

1. Record several specific blessings you've received from reading (or hearing) God's Word.

2. The Word of God is to the soul what food is to the body. Based on your intake of the Word in recent months, how well-nourished are you spiritually?

3. Evaluate your current approach to reading Scripture.

    - Do you read *prayerfully*? Are you conscious of your dependence on the Holy Spirit to give you understanding? Do you read the Word with the intent to obey whatever God shows you?

    - Do you read *thoughtfully*? Do you take time to meditate on the meaning of what you're reading? Do you "store God's Word up in your heart" by memorizing Scripture (see Ps. 119:11)?

    - Do you read *systematically*? Are you getting a balanced spiritual diet by taking in the whole of God's Word? Do you have a plan for reading the Bible to help you avoid overlooking certain portions?

4. If you don't already have a plan for regular Bible reading, ask the Lord to help you determine where and how to start. Record what He puts on your heart.

   When will you set aside time in the next twenty-four hours to begin reading?

5. If you're already in the habit of reading Scripture, are you just going through an intellectual exercise (as the Pharisees did), or are you truly getting to know the Lord through His Word? If this aspect of your study is lacking, what changes might you need to make?

CHAPTER 9

Getting the Word into You

Have you ever had the experience of reading a portion of Scripture—perhaps even several pages or chapters—only to stop and realize that you have absolutely no idea what you just read? That has happened to me more times than I care to admit.

Or perhaps you find it difficult to concentrate when you're reading the Word. Your eyes may be seeing words about the children of Israel in the wilderness or Jesus and His disciples in a boat, but your mind is thinking about the text you just received from your mother-in-law, your annual performance review scheduled for that afternoon, your kids' upcoming weekend with their dad and his girlfriend, or a thousand other things that have nothing to do with what you're reading.

We've talked about the value and necessity of reading God's Word. That's the starting place in getting to know God. As Spurgeon said, "If you wish to know God you must know His Word."[1] Now I want to suggest a practical step that will help make the Word bear even more fruit in your life. This practice will help you concentrate on what you're reading and can breathe new life into your devotional time. You may begin to find that you truly don't want to miss a single day of spending time in the Word.

> God never intended that we should merely get into His Word. His intent has always been that the Word should get into us.

Keep in mind that it's not enough that we should just *read* the Word. The goal is for the words that are printed on the page to become written on our hearts.

God never intended that we should merely get into His Word. His intent has always been that the Word should get into us.

So how do we go about getting the Word grafted into our hearts and lives? Here's one key.

WRITE AS YOU READ

Next to the Holy Spirit, one of the greatest helps in my personal devotional life has been to read the Bible with some means of recording observations and responses, whether handwritten or digital notes. As I do, the words of Scripture become fuel for fresh wonder, worship, and obedience.

This process doesn't have to be difficult or complex. In fact, over the years I've challenged some of my friends' kids to read through the Bible and write down two sentences about every chapter: one sentence summarizing the chapter and another with a personal takeaway for their life. Even this simple approach can be enormously beneficial. But there are several other types of writing that can enhance our study of the Word, most of them illustrated in the Scripture itself.

These tools, which have been useful to me, are simply ideas to get you started on your own journey. Find out which methods work best for you and use them. As long as you're getting into the Word and the Word is getting into you, you're doing it right!

Write Out Portions of the Word

Prior to the invention of the printing press, people did not have their own copies of the Bible. It was painstakingly copied out by hand and passed on from one generation to the next. And while I'm not longing to return to those days, I believe something precious may have been lost for those of us who can so easily purchase a printed version of the Word of God—a benefit that comes with copying out portions word for word.

On several occasions in the Old Testament God instructed people to do this very thing. When Moses went up on the mountain to meet with God, the Lord said to him, "'Write these words....' And he wrote on the tablets the words of the covenant, the Ten Commandments" (Ex. 34:27–28).

Forty years later, as the children of Israel were preparing to enter the Promised Land, Moses rehearsed God's laws for the entire congregation and then instructed them: "You shall write them on the doorposts of your house and on your gates" (Deut. 6:9). (This verse has motivated me to display Scripture throughout my house. These pieces, whether on walls or other surfaces, serve as visual reminders of the ways of God, as well as ministering to others who visit in my home.)

Shortly before his death, Moses once again called the Israelites together and told them that after they crossed the Jordan River and entered Canaan they were to select some large stones, set them up on Mount Ebal (about thirty-five miles north of Jerusalem), and "write on the stones all the words of this law very plainly" (Deut. 27:8).

Earlier we saw the instruction God gave to the kings of Israel:

> When he sits on the throne of his kingdom, he shall write for himself in a book a copy of this law.... And it shall be with him, and he shall read in it all the days of his life. (Deut. 17:18–19)

What was the point of this exercise? Do you remember in elementary school when the teacher would instruct the class to copy a page out of a textbook or a list from the chalkboard (or, if you're younger than I am, a whiteboard or smartboard)? It may have seemed like meaningless busywork to you. But the teacher knew that if you wrote out the material for yourself, you were more likely to grasp and remember the concepts.

God knew how prone His people were to forget what He had told them, even the things He'd repeated over and over. He challenged them to "remember" Him, to remember His law, to remember what He had done for them. Having them write out the Word of God was one practical way to help them remember.

It can help us remember as well. Taking time to write out specific passages from the Word forces us to think about what we're reading and to observe the details of the text more carefully.

I know many people who have found this helpful. One friend shared with me the blessing he received from copying out the Gospel of Luke. Another friend copies paragraphs of the Bible onto three-by-five cards and then memorizes and meditates on those passages each morning while running on the treadmill. Over the course of several years, a young colleague wrote out the entire Bible by hand. Recently I met an older man who has been doing the same since his wife was taken to heaven a few years ago. He shared the great comfort this practice has provided for him in this difficult season.

Write in Your Bible

This suggestion is not specifically found in the Scripture—remember that hardly anyone owned a copy of the Bible before the sixteenth century—but it has been a practical help and blessing in my lifelong love affair with the Word. When I was a child, my parents encouraged us to underline verses that we found especially meaningful, and that practice stuck with me. (At one point, I got carried away with the idea, leading my dad to suggest that perhaps I should underline only those verses that were not particularly meaningful to me!)

Over more than sixty years, I have read and marked up dozens of different Bibles. Each one tells a story of my personal faith journey during a particular time period. In addition to underlining phrases or verses for emphasis, I frequently circle or bracket repeated words or phrases. I also write down cross-references (more about this later) and jot down notes about the meaning of specific words or phrases in the passage.

When the Lord uses a verse or passage to address a specific

need in my life or to encourage or convict my heart in an unusual way, I often record in my Bible the date (and sometimes the place). The space in the margins is sometimes used to write brief, personal responses to the truth: "Yes, Lord," "I agree," "Change my heart, O God," or "Make this true in my life, Lord."

Write in a Devotional Journal

This can be a way of engaging even more deeply with the Lord and His Word. It has been a rich blessing and a significant part of my spiritual growth for many years.

Over the years, I've filled scores of journals with observations and insights from reading and meditating on the Word. Capturing these thoughts helps me clarify, understand, and remember the ways of God. The process of writing them down deepens my love and appreciation for the truth of God's Word. The journal you use could be anything from a school-type spiral to a commercially produced blank book—but I personally find it helpful to have lined pages. Alternatively, you may prefer to use a digital journal.

In addition to my "standalone" journals, I've also enjoyed using Bibles designed specifically to be written in. These Bibles are formatted to allow plenty of extra space for notes, responses, journaling, even artwork. The five-year period I spent journaling my way through the *CSB Notetaking Bible* was a highlight of my Christian journey and deeply increased my love for the Word.[2] I can't recommend this concept highly enough.

WHAT GOES IN A DEVOTIONAL JOURNAL?

Each time I make an entry in my devotional journal, I record the date and the passage I'm reading. There is no "right" way to do devotional journaling. But many Bible teachers suggest asking three basic questions as we read and meditate on the Scripture.

- *What does it say? (Make observations about the text.)*
- *What does it mean? (Look for the implications or the interpretation of the text.)*
- *What should I do? (Make practical application of the text.)*

Let's unpack each of those a bit further.

What Does It Say? (Observation)

This quote attributed to Martin Luther suggests a useful way to learn what a passage is saying:

> I study my Bible as I gather apples. First, I shake the whole tree that the ripest may fall. Then I shake each limb, and when I have shaken each limb, I shake each branch and every twig. Then I look under every leaf.[3]

Luther was suggesting that we should start with the simplest, most obvious observations about the text and then probe more deeply for further understanding.

Here are some ways you can make observations about what the Scripture is actually saying. (If you happen to be a firstborn like me who thinks you've got to check off each item on a list like this, remember, these are just suggestions to prime the pump. Use whichever ones are helpful and save the others for another time.)

1. *Summarize.* After reading the passage, try to come up with a title for the entire book, the chapter, and the individual paragraphs. Look for a key verse that captures the heart of the passage. Write a brief summary overview of the passage, including the major points.

2. *Paraphrase.* Rewrite the passage in your own words.

3. *Ask questions.* Use the kinds of questions a journalist might ask:

   - *Who* wrote it? Said it? About whom? Speaking to whom?

   - *What* happened? What are the main events? The major ideas? The theme?

   - *When* was it written? Did the events already take place? Will they happen in the future?

   - *Where* did (or will) this happen?

   - *Why* was this written? (Sometimes the answer will be right in the text, as in John 20:31 and 1 John 5:13.)

   - *How* did it happen? Is it still happening?

Write down any additional questions that the passage raises in your mind. You may not be able to come up with the answers right away, but often you'll find that other passages will provide the answers you're looking for.

4. *Look for patterns.* Look for repeated words or phrases to help you understand what the author intended to emphasize. For example:

- As you read the book of Leviticus, circle the words *holy, clean, unclean,* and related words every time they appear. Then summarize what this book teaches about holiness.

- In the book of 1 John, highlight the repeated phrase, "by *this we know*" to help you make a list of evidences of genuine salvation.

- In 1 Peter, mark every reference to *suffering* and *glory* to see the connection between the two. *Submission* is another recurring theme in 1 Peter. Make a note of each relationship where someone is to be submissive.

- In Ezekiel, variations of the phrase, "*know that I am the* L*ORD*" appear nearly fifty times in forty-eight chapters. What does that tell you about God's purposes in our world?

- In the book of Hebrews, Jesus is said to be "superior to angels (1:4) and "worthy of more glory than Moses (3:3), and His ministry is said to be "much more excellent than" that of the Old Testament priests (8:6). What is the common theme here?

5. *Look for cross-references.* As you become more familiar with the Bible, you will find that as you read a passage, the Holy Spirit will bring to mind other verses that relate to, confirm, or shed further light on what you're reading. For example, Daniel 5:17 records that Daniel refused to accept the payment that King Belshazzar offered him for interpreting the writing on the wall. That brings to mind two other passages where godly men did the same thing (Elisha–2 Kings 5:16; Abraham–Genesis

14:21–24). God used these passages to caution me about the danger of ministering for personal or material gain.

6. *Make use of study tools.* You'll find the following resources helpful as you seek to discover what a passage is saying. Virtually all of them are available in book form as well as online and in digital apps.

- *An English dictionary* is useful for looking up the basic meaning of words. Noah Webster's original *1828 Dictionary* gives rich, biblical definitions of many English words such as *grace, faith, repentance,* and *blessing.*[4]

- *Various translations* of the Bible can shed fresh light on passages and help in understanding their meaning. Excellent translations include the English Standard Version, New King James Version, Christian Standard Bible, and the New American Standard Bible.[5]

- *A concordance* is helpful for doing word studies, finding all the places a word is used in the Bible, and discovering which word in the original language is being translated in the English Bible. Strong's Exhaustive Concordance is a classic in this category.[6] You may also want to find a concordance specifically keyed to the version of the Bible you use the most.[7]

- *A Bible dictionary* can help you understand the meaning and usage of specific words in the English Bible. *Vine's Expository Dictionary* is one I refer to frequently.

- *Commentaries and study Bibles* can be helpful in understanding difficult passages or gaining background on such things as biblical authors, locations, characters, and customs. However, these tools aren't a good substitute for your own reading, meditation, and study of the passage. God has given you His Holy Spirit to help you understand His Word. Commentaries and study Bible notes are not divinely inspired; they are merely the work of men and women who have sought to understand and explain the Word.[8]

The internet offers a wealth of information. I frequently use my phone to look up cross-references, alternate versions, and Hebrew or Greek original words, to check commentaries on particular verses, and so on. And I know some people prefer to read an online Bible and/or to take notes on a digital device.

The challenge for me is to avoid those all-too-familiar distractions that can come with having a device close at hand. It's so easy to get drawn into a digital rabbit hole while looking something up or to succumb to the temptation to check email or scroll social media feeds. Technology can be more of a hindrance than a help to me when it comes to spending focused time alone with the Lord. Perhaps you've found that to be true as well.

> *Constant, prayerful, vigilant attention to our habits and the heart out of which those habits flow is a must. Otherwise, we'll end up bowing to the authority of algorithms rather than to the Almighty.*

If there's a one-size-fits-all formula for dealing with this important issue, I've not discovered it yet. What I know is that constant, prayerful, vigilant attention to our habits and the heart out of which those habits flow is a must. Otherwise, we'll end up bowing to the authority of algorithms rather than to the Almighty.

What Does It Mean? *(Implications/Interpretation)*

In addition to the questions you've asked to help determine what the passage says, as you read the Bible ask questions like these to help you interpret the text:

- What does this passage teach me about God, His attributes, His character, His works?
- What does it teach about human nature? About the consequences of sin or disobedience?
- Does this passage point ahead to Jesus, His mission, His saving ministry or fulfill any Old Testament prophecies?
- What does this passage reveal show about salvation, grace, or faith?
- Are there any word pictures or cultural elements that reflect deeper spiritual truths?
- Are there any promises to claim? How does this passage encourage trust in God's faithfulness?
- Are there any commands to obey?
- Are there any examples to follow? Sins to avoid?
- What does it teach about God's perspective on priorities, values, or attitudes?
- Does this passage confront wrong thinking or false beliefs?
- How does it encourage an eternal perspective?

What Should I Do? (Response and Application)

One pastor whose sermons I listened to occasionally years ago began each message by opening up a specific text of Scripture and explaining what it says and what it means. Then he would come to a certain point in each message where he would make the statement: "That's the *what*. Now, the question is: *So what?*" That pastor wasn't satisfied for his listeners just to know *what* the passage said—as important as that was. He wanted to be sure they also made practical application of the truth to their lives. In addition to these two questions, I like to ask: *What now?* Is there a specific step of action I need to take?

This need for this progression is seen throughout Scripture. God told Ezekiel that the problem with His people was that "they sit before you as my people, and they hear what you say but they will not do it" (Ezek. 33:31).

Hebrews 4:2 tells us that "the message [the children of Israel] heard did not benefit them, because they were not united by faith with those who listened"—that is, they didn't act on what they heard.

The book of James makes the same point: "Do not merely listen to the word, and so deceive yourselves. *Do what it says*" (James 1:22 NIV).

The old-time evangelist Rodney "Gipsy" Smith is quoted as saying, "What makes the difference is not how many times you have been through the Bible, but how many times and how thoroughly the Bible has been through you."[9]

As you meditate on the Scripture, ask such questions as:

- How does this truth apply to my life? To my current situation?

- In view of this truth, what changes do I need to make?
- What practical steps can I take to apply this truth to my life?

Everything we read in God's Word calls for some type of response. That response may include:

- exercising faith in God's promises or character
- humbling ourselves and acknowledging our need
- confessing sin
- turning from our old ways of thinking
- obeying a command we've been neglecting
- worshiping and adoring the God who has revealed Himself
- forgiving someone who has wronged us
- seeking forgiveness from someone we have wronged
- seeking to reconcile a broken relationship
- giving to meet the need of another
- sharing the good news of Jesus Christ with a non-Christian friend or relative
- interceding on behalf of a needy friend

Recording your responses to His Word will help move you past simply *hearing* the Word to *doing* it. You may want to write out your response in the form of a prayer expressing your commitment to the Lord. Another helpful step is to share with a friend what God has put on your heart and ask her to help hold you accountable to obey the Lord.

The book of Nehemiah describes a great revival that God sent to the exiles who had returned to Israel from captivity in Babylon. The revival was birthed when the congregation gathered together to listen to Ezra the priest read the Word of God in a service that lasted most of the day, continued for another seven days, and then resumed two weeks later.

The ninth chapter of Nehemiah records a long prayer of corporate confession made by the repentant Israelites. The prayer concludes with these words: "Because of this we make a firm covenant *in writing*" (v. 38). Nehemiah 10 goes on to record the details of the covenant they made that day. It includes promises to obey God in such matters as marriage, Sabbath observance, and tithing. By writing out and signing this covenant, they became more accountable for their response to the Word they had heard.

My devotional journals and the margins of my Bibles include many such responses to the Word of God. Some are in the form of prayers—prayers of thanksgiving, praise, confession, repentance, intercession, or supplication.

On one occasion, for example, I recorded the following response to Jesus' teaching about forgiveness in Matthew 18:23–35:

> How often I am like that forgiven servant who refused to forgive in turn, but instead demanded payment from his fellow servant, who owed him a pittance.
> O Father, You have had compassion on me and loosed me from the infinite debt of sin. Yet sometimes I still insist on taking my fellow servants "by the

throat," dealing roughly with them and insisting that they fulfill some relatively small obligation to me.

Forgive me for not treating others with the same compassion I have received from You. May I be as generous in dispensing grace to others as You have been with me.

In the book of Joshua we read about an encounter between Joshua and a heavenly messenger (most likely a preincarnate manifestation of Christ). When Joshua looked up and saw the stranger standing before him with a drawn sword in his hand, Joshua approached him to find out whose side he was on. Instead of answering directly, the warrior identified himself as "the commander of the army of the LORD." And Joshua's response was immediate:

> [He] fell on his face to the earth and worshiped and said to him, "What does my lord say to his servant?" And the commander of the Lord's army said to Joshua, "Take off your sandals from your feet, for the place where you are standing is holy." And Joshua did so. (Josh. 5:14–15)

Notice the progression here: The Lord approached Joshua. And as soon as Joshua realized who was speaking to him, he humbled himself and asked, "What do you want to say to me?" He listened carefully to the Lord's words and then immediately obeyed.

This issue of obedience to the Word of God is crucial in cultivating a close relationship with God—the kind of relationship described in this prayer by Spurgeon:

> Lord, may Thy Word be the supreme ruler of our being. May we give ourselves up to its sacred law to be obedient to its every hint, wishing in all things,

even in the least things, to do the will of God from the heart and having every thought brought into captivity to the mind of the Spirit of God.[10]

What Has God Been Doing in My Life? (Spiritual Milestones)

In addition to journaling insights and responses related to what I've read in the Word, I also take time on occasion to record significant markers in my walk with God. (I may use a separate section of my journal or a different journal altogether for these notes. Or I may interject them into my regular journaling.) These entries, along with my ongoing responses to whatever Scripture I'm reading, become chronicles of what God has been doing in my life—a faith-building record of growth and discovery I can look back on and learn from.

This practice of marking important spiritual milestones has precedent in Scripture. Shortly after the children of Israel were delivered out of Egypt, they were attacked by a fierce band of Amalekites. On the day of the battle, Joshua, Moses' young lieutenant, led the Israelite army out to face the enemy. This was to be the eager young leader's first battle, with Moses overseeing. When the battle was ready to begin down in the valley, Moses walked to the top of a nearby hill, grasped his shepherd's rod ("the rod of God") with both hands, and raised his hands up to heaven. What happened next is recorded for us in some detail in Exodus chapter 17:

> Whenever Moses held up his hand, Israel prevailed, and whenever he lowered his hand, Amalek prevailed. But Moses' hands grew weary, so they took a stone and put it under him, and he sat on it, while Aaron and Hur held up his hands, one on one side, and

the other on the other side. So his hands were steady until the going down of the sun. And Joshua overwhelmed Amalek and his people with the sword. (Ex. 17:11–13)

End of battle, end of story, right?

Well, not quite.

God didn't want Joshua ever to forget the lessons of that day—that the Amalekites were His eternal enemies and that the Lord alone had the power to overcome them. So God said to Moses, "Write this as a memorial in a book and recite it in the ears of Joshua" (Ex. 17:14). This is perhaps the first biblical illustration of what many today call "journaling."

You wouldn't think Joshua could ever forget what had just taken place that day—any more than we could forget the times that God moved in a significant way in our lives. But God, who understands human frailty, knew how faulty our memories can be. He wanted to be sure that, even when Joshua was an old man with lots of victories under his belt, he would have a permanent record of this particular battle—a written reminder of the true Source of his power.

That unusual battle wasn't the only time Moses made a "journal entry." Throughout the forty years that the children of Israel wandered in the wilderness, Moses kept a record of the Lord's dealings with His people. Why? Because God told him to. "At the LORD's command Moses recorded the stages in their journey" (Num. 33:2 NIV).

I think there were at least three reasons God told Moses to keep this journal: (1) so the Israelites would remember what they had learned of the heart and ways of God at each stage of the journey; (2) so their children might learn the same lessons; and (3) so we, too, could learn from their experiences. In fact, the New Testament makes two specific references to Moses' journal:

> "For everything that was written in the past was written to teach us, so that through endurance and the encouragement of the Scriptures we might have hope." (Rom. 15:4)

> "These things ... were written down as warnings for us." (1 Cor. 10:11)

My own experience confirms the Bible's wisdom in this regard. I gain understanding and encouragement both in the process of recording spiritual milestones and in reading back over what I have written over the years, tracing the progress of God's work in my life. While what I record may center around specific circumstances in my life, invariably it is birthed out of the Scripture, as the Spirit uses whatever I may be reading at that time to shed light on my path. For example, the following was written shortly after the unexpected death of a beloved spiritual mentor. It was a response to Psalm 146:

> The deepest needs of my life cannot be met by any created being, but only by God Himself. Those human instruments that I have looked to in the past for help have now died, as the Word says they will (vv. 3–4). They can no longer help me. So, dear Father, I look to You to meet my needs. "Blessed is he whose help is the God of Jacob, whose hope is in the Lord his God" (v. 5). "Whom have I in heaven but you? And there is nothing on earth that I desire besides you." (Ps. 73:25)

In the Old Testament, God instructed His people to observe a series of specific feasts each year. Each of these feasts represented some aspect of God's redemptive plan. In fact, that is where the whole concept of "holidays" (that is, "holy days") originated. In my own life, I have tried to set aside time on special days (both my natural and spiritual birthdays, the beginning of a new year, and so on) to meditate on God's goodness and to seek His face. One lengthy journal entry, a prayer written on my thirty-fifth birthday, reads in part:

> As I look ahead to another year of life, I am reminded that I may not spend another year here on this earth. Within that space, You may call me to heaven, or the Lord Jesus may return for His Bride. "Teach [me] to number [my] days and recognize how few they are; help [me] to spend them as [I] should" (Ps. 90:12 TLB).
>
> Help me to live whatever days I have remaining in light of eternity. I humbly seek Your blessing and Your favor, for having them, I lack nothing. I would seek to please You rather than men. This year I ask
>
> – to know and love You in ever-increasing intimacy
>
> – for the protection of Your Spirit over my heart, my mind, and my affections
>
> – that You would keep me from sin and from the evil one
>
> – to be faithful in fulfilling the ministry You have entrusted to me—faithful in small tasks as well as large, in secret and obscurity as well as in public
>
> – for a heart full of love for others
>
> – that You would make me fruitful
>
> – that every day might be lived to the fullest and in the constant, conscious awareness of Your presence
>
> – that I might walk in the light before You and others, without guile or pretense
>
> – that I might be holy and humble before You and others

GETTING THE WORD INTO YOU

"I SAW WITH MY OWN EYES": THE POWER OF GETTING THE WORD INTO YOU

Three thousand years ago, an Arabian queen learned of a foreign king whose achievements and wisdom were legendary. Determined to see for herself, she gathered together a large caravan carrying rare and expensive gifts and then traveled twelve hundred miles to meet the monarch.

Upon her arrival the Queen of Sheba was warmly welcomed by the king. He listened as she told him all that was on her mind and asked many difficult questions, all of which he answered willingly and easily. When she saw the vast wealth and wisdom of the king, the queen was overcome. She said to the king,

> The report was true that I heard in my own land of your words and of your wisdom, but I did not believe the reports *until I came and my own eyes had seen it.* And behold, the half was not told me. Your wisdom and prosperity surpass the report that I heard. Happy are your men! Happy are your servants, who continually stand before you and hear your wisdom! (1 Kings 10:6–8)

The Queen of Sheba brought many fine gifts from her homeland to Solomon. But she did not leave his court empty-handed:

> King Solomon gave [her] all that she desired, whatever she asked besides what she had brought to the king. (2 Chron. 9:12)

It's one thing to listen to others speak of the wonders of King Jesus. It is quite another to make the effort to go and meet Him for yourself—to see firsthand His vast stores of wealth, to ask Him your hard questions, to share all that is on your heart, and to listen intently as He shares with you the secrets of His kingdom. When you have met Him in this way, you will understand why His servants consider it their highest joy to stand before Him each day and hear His wisdom.

And when you go back to your place—your home, your job, your neighborhood—you will not go empty-handed. You will return with more than your hands and heart can contain. For He will give you all the desires of your heart—far more than you ever could have brought to Him.

Have you been relying on secondhand reports about the greatness of God? Why not "taste and see" for yourself "that the LORD is good" (Ps. 34:8)?

A number of years ago I received the following testimony from a woman who did just that. You can sense the great joy she experienced as she learned how to get into the Word and get the Word into her life.

> Last fall I attended a women's retreat where you taught the entire book of the Song of Solomon. You paralleled the bride and the bridegroom's relationship to our relationship with the Lord. You pointed out that when the bride first lost her beloved she wasn't willing to venture out from her bed to search for him (Song of Solomon 3:1). God showed me that this was true in my own life. I wasn't willing to journey into God's Word to seek Him, thus building a strong relationship with Him. Most of my growth had come because of someone else's hard work. If I needed help in a certain area, I would read a book or listen to a sermon on the subject.
>
> I am not saying I never read my Bible, because I did. But reading my Bible and studying God's Word are not the same. I was unbalanced. The following analogy helped me understand the difference.
>
> I love to shop in those aroma-filled grocery stores. Fresh bread is baked in big ovens. Wonderful smells lure you to the bakery

counter, and you can't resist. At dinner that evening you pass real butter and fresh bread. Everyone goes, "Mmmmmm!" Did you enjoy that bread? I sure did. Did you do the work of preparing it? No. Was it wrong to enjoy it because you didn't do the work? Again, no!

Now consider this scene. Again you are at the store, only this time you buy flour, yeast, eggs, butter, and milk. At home you pull out a large bowl, measuring utensils, a few pans, your ingredients, and a cookbook. Now you start your own aromas drifting. Your home, not the store, smells wonderful. You are filled with a sense of satisfaction as you set the beautiful loaf of golden-brown bread on the table. Your family says, "Wow! Did you make that?"

Which bread did you enjoy more? Digging a truth from God's Word on your own gives you a real sense of accomplishment, just as making fresh bread would.

When I left the retreat I knew what change had to take place in my life. I would have to begin a consistent study of God's Word. How was I to accomplish this, since I had depended on others for so long? Trusting God to show me, I prayed and asked the Lord what to study.

Presently I am doing word studies. These have caused real growth in my life. One morning I used a Strong's Concordance and a Thompson Chain Reference Bible to study the word *revenge*. Using these tools I traced the word through Scripture. I learned much about *revenge* and words of a similar nature, such as *vengeance* in Romans 12:19.

When I went outside that morning, I discovered that someone had pelted our newly painted tan garage with ripe cherries. Then they walked around the house and let the freshly primed windows have it. What surprised me more than the cherries was my reaction. Soap and water in hand, I began to wash it off. I didn't even get angry. What a victory to learn we aren't to desire revenge and then to see it worked out in my own life.

That was a dramatic example of what I have learned. Every day doesn't bring forth such powerful results. But as I reflect on the past year, I realize the groping is gone. I am a stronger Christian because of studying God's Word for myself.

MAKE IT PERSONAL

The "Make It Personal" section for this chapter is longer than usual. It's intended to help you put into practice what you've learned in this chapter by guiding you as you meditate on a specific passage from God's Word. You may want to set aside some extended time over the next several days in order to get the most out of this section.

1. Read Psalm 19. Ask God to speak to you through this familiar passage and to make it fresh to your heart.

    a. In your journal, write out the entire psalm, word for word.

    b. Record *observations* about this passage ("What does it *say?*"). Here are some suggestions you may want to use:

    - *Summarize.* What title would you give to this selection of Scripture? Divide the psalm into two or more sections and suggest a title for each. Write a one-paragraph summary or overview of the passage.

    - *Paraphrase.* Write out the psalm in your own words.

    - *Ask questions.* Who wrote this psalm? Why did he write it? What is the connection between "the heavens" (vv. 1–6) and "the law of the Lord" (vv. 7–11)? How are they alike? What synonyms are used in this passage for the Word of God? What adjectives does the author use to describe the Word of God? What benefits and blessings does the Word bring to our lives? What two kinds of sins does the author pray to be delivered from (vv. 12–13)? What does the psalmist want the Word of God to accomplish in his life?

- *Look for patterns.* What pattern do you see in the four parallel lines of vv. 7–8?

- *Look for cross-references.* Using a concordance, the references in the margin of your Bible, or your memory, list four Scripture references that relate to specific phrases in Psalm 19. (For example, relate Prov. 8:19 to Ps. 19:10.)

- *Use study tools.* Select a word or phrase from this psalm that you would like to understand better. Use one of the tools recommended in this chapter (English dictionary, alternate translation(s), a concordance, a Bible dictionary, or commentary) to gain further insight on that word or phrase.

c. Record some of the *implications* of this passage ("What does it *mean?*"). Consider the following types of questions:

- Why is the Word of God so vital and valuable to the child of God?

- What are some consequences we may experience if the Word of God is not kept central in our daily lives?

- Why does the Word of God not produce the desired results in the life of every believer?

- God promises "great reward" to those who keep His Word (v. 11). What does it mean to keep His Word? What might some of those rewards be?

- How does the Word of God help protect us from sin?

d. Record specific, practical *applications* that the Holy Spirit helps you make from this passage ("What should I *do*?"). Seek to engraft this passage into your life using one or more of the following suggestions:

- Which of the benefits and blessings in verses 7–11 would you like to experience in a greater measure? The Word of God is designed to accomplish these results in our lives. What practical steps can you take to make the Word a higher priority in your life?

- Are you aware of anything in the Word of God that you are not currently obeying? What do you need to do to repent of going your own way and to begin walking in obedience to His Word?

- Pray aloud the prayer of the psalmist in verses 12–13. Then express the same prayer in your own words.

- Select one key verse from this psalm; memorize that verse and meditate on it over the next twenty-four hours.

- Write a prayer expressing to God your desire to feast on His Word and to have it engrafted into your life.

- Share with a friend or family member what God has said to you through this passage. Ask that individual to hold you accountable for any specific steps of action the Lord has laid on your heart.

2. Choose one of the following exercises to record milestones in your spiritual pilgrimage:

   a. Name some of the individuals who have had the greatest influence on your walk with God. How have they impacted your life? Record your answers in your journal.

   b. Record the spiritual highlights of the past year. What major events or circumstances have you walked through? What have you learned from each about the heart and ways of God?

   c. Choose three or four attributes of God and record a specific instance in your life in which God has demonstrated each of those qualities.

d. Write a three- to five-page "spiritual autobiography," summarizing how you came to faith in Christ and highlighting key stages of your spiritual pilgrimage and growth.

PART FIVE
SECTION TWO

Responding to His Word

Mary ... anointed the feet of Jesus.
JOHN 12:3

After a very few minutes my soul has been led to confession, or to thanksgiving, or to intercession, or to supplication.... When thus I have been for a while making confession or intercession or supplication, or have given thanks, I go on to the next words or verse, turning all, as I go on, into prayer for myself or others, as the Word may lead to it....

The result of this is that there is always a good deal of confession, thanksgiving, supplication, or intercession mingled with my meditation, and that my inner man almost invariably is even sensibly nourished and strengthened, and that by breakfast time, with rare exceptions, I am in a peaceful if not happy state of heart.

GEORGE MÜLLER

CHAPTER 10

The Perfume of Praise

"He is aliiiiive! He is aliiiiive!"
It was Easter Sunday morning. My five-year-old nephew was to be baptized that day. My mother had flown into town to share in the occasion. As the family was getting ready for church, she heard little Mookie's unmistakable voice coming from the bathroom down the hall. She quietly slipped into the hallway and peeked into the bath to see what was happening. There stood the child on a stepstool in front of the mirror, carefully combing his hair, then straightening his shirt and pants, while singing at the top of his lungs, totally oblivious to anyone who might be listening in as he joyously serenaded the Lord.

Children sometimes have a way of grasping things that grown-ups miss.

Take the time that children shouted out praises to Jesus in the temple. It was the week before the Passover. The temple was busy with people making last-minute purchases. Incensed by the corruption and crass commercialism taking place in what was intended to be a house of worship and prayer, Jesus had just made quite a scene by driving the money changers and merchants from the outer court of the temple. Now He was attracting attention by healing the blind and the lame—outcasts who normally were not even allowed in the temple. To make matters worse, the children who had seen it all were loudly acclaiming Him as the Messiah. "Hosanna to the Son of David!" they cried out.

That did it. Those religious leaders had had more than they could take. Matthew tells us that when they "saw the wonderful things that he did, and the children crying out in the temple . . . they were indignant, and they said to him, 'Do you hear what these are saying?'" (Matt. 21:15–16). The implication: "Make them stop!"

Get the picture? The chief priests and teachers of the law were the ones who were supposed to be experts in worship. But instead of encouraging the people to worship God, they were busy running a lucrative business. When Jesus had compassion on the sick and demonstrated His power by healing them, and when the children responded in simple, heartfelt worship, those same leaders got upset and moved in to put a stop to the whole thing.

When the children saw the wonderful things Jesus did, they worshiped—which is what you were supposed to do in the temple! But when the temple leaders saw the wonderful things Jesus did, they worried about the religious and political implications of what was happening. What if this man, lauded by the people as the Messiah, toppled their centuries-old religious system? And what if the whole commotion antagonized the local Roman authorities?

The children shouted out their praises without inhibition,

while the leaders feared that things might get out of control—their control, that is. The children were preoccupied with Jesus; they were not the least bit conscious of how others saw them or what anyone else was thinking. The leaders, on the other hand, were concerned about how they looked, about holding on to their position, about what everyone else would think about this whole scene.

And the children had it right. The grown-ups had it wrong.

Responding to God

We've considered the necessity and delight of getting into the Word of God and getting His Word into us. We've seen that it's through the Word that we come to know God— His heart, His ways, His character, His eternal purposes and plan. Now we turn our attention to *responding* to what God reveals to us in His Word.

As our loving, heavenly Father, God wants to speak to us—which requires that we learn to be still and listen to His Word. But He also wants to have two-way communication with us, much as we long for communication with our family and friends to go both ways. When you call a friend to share a piece of exciting news, you hope she'll respond, that she'll share in your enthusiasm. When you express your love to your husband, you want to know that he's heard you and to be reassured of his love for you. When you present a much-anticipated gift to one of your children, you're delighted to hear, "Thanks, Mom!"

In the same way, God delights in our response to Him. And praise (or worship) is one of the most basic ways we can respond to what He reveals to us through His Word.

Exodus 14 gives us the dramatic account of God's parting the waters of the Red Sea so that His people might be delivered from the Egyptian army. What was the response of Moses and the Israelites to this great display of God's redemptive power? They responded with worship and praise:

> I will sing to the LORD, for he has triumphed gloriously;
> the horse and his rider he has thrown into the sea.
> The LORD is my strength and my song,
> and he has become my salvation;
> this is my God, and I will praise him,
> my father's God, and I will exalt him. (Ex. 15:1–2)

When Jesus revealed His power and grace by cleansing ten desperate lepers, "one of them, when he saw that he was healed, turned back, praising God with a loud voice; and he fell on his face at Jesus' feet, giving him thanks" (Luke 17:15–16). The fact that nine of the ten failed to return to give thanks did not go unnoticed by Jesus who asked with amazement, "Was no one found to return and give praise to God except this foreigner?" (v. 18).

And then, of course, there was Mary of Bethany. Of all the human relationships Jesus had while on this earth, the one He shared with Mary stands out in terms of devotion.

When we first meet Mary, she is in her home, sitting at Jesus' feet, waiting quietly in His presence (Luke 10:38–42—the "Mary and Martha" story). Sometime later, when Jesus arrives in Bethany just after her brother's death, we find Mary clinging to His feet, weeping over the enormous loss she has just experienced (John 11:32–33). And when we encounter Mary again, she is once more at the feet of Jesus, this time worshiping the One she has come to know, trust,

THE PERFUME OF PRAISE

and adore with an act of stunning—and costly—worship.

You see, Mary was not satisfied just to *receive* from Jesus. As she listened to His heart, she longed to *respond* to Him—to give back to Him, as He had given to her. Three of the Gospels record Mary's most poignant response to the love He had shown her (Matt. 26:6–13; Mark 14:3–9; John 12:1–8).[1]

Mary had lingered in Jesus' presence. She had listened to His words. She had learned from His life and experienced His unconditional love for her.

> Mary was not satisfied just to receive from Jesus. As she listened to His heart, she longed to respond to Him— to give back to Him, as He had given to her.

And worship was the natural response of her grateful heart. Oblivious to the curious stares and irate mumbling of the onlookers, Mary showed her love by pouring out an expensive container of sweet-smelling ointment on His feet and His head and then wiping up the excess with her hair.

No one who was present that day could escape the impact of this woman's deed. Matthew's account tells us that the disciples "were indignant, saying. 'Why this waste?'" (Matt. 26:8). To those men, Mary's act seemed over-the-top extravagant, for they did not understand the infinite worth of worship.

On the other hand, Jesus, who was the object of Mary's devotion, was pleased. "She has done a beautiful thing to me," He responded to the bothered disciples (v. 10).

Significantly, Mary's worship also had an unintended effect on her. As she anointed Jesus' feet with the precious ointment and then wiped His feet with her hair, she became fragrant with the very perfume she had lavished on Him.

Further, John tells us that "the house was filled with the fragrance of the perfume" (John 12:3).

When you and I sit at Jesus' feet and listen to His Word, then respond by lavishing our worship and love upon Him, there will be an impact. Some may not understand. They may even object. And yet true worship and devotion will make our lives fragrant and will perfume the environment around us with praise. Our homes, our churches, even our places of work will bear the sweet scent of our response to God.

Most important, the Lord Jesus will be pleased.

And that, of course, is what matters most.

What Is Worship?

Worship is our response to God's revelation of Himself. It is expressing wonder, awe, and gratitude for His greatness and goodness. It is the appropriate response to His person, His provision, His power, His promises, and His plan.

Praise and thanksgiving are two important dimensions of worship. Praise is verbal or visible adoration of God for who He is. Thanksgiving involves expressing gratitude for what He has done. Praise focuses on the Giver, while thanksgiving acknowledges His gifts.

The Scripture does not make a strong distinction between praise, worship, and thanksgiving—they can all be considered an appropriate response to what we have come to know of God through His Word. In the pages to come, we will look first at some general biblical principles regarding praise. Then we'll explore some practical ways we can express praise in our daily time alone with the Lord.

WHY PRAISE?

The Bible gives us a number of different reasons why praise is such an important part of our relationship with God and why we should engage in it. First, and most basic, we should praise the Lord because *He commands us to praise Him.* Did you know that the most frequently repeated command in all of God's Word is the command to "praise the Lord"? (I suspect it may also be the most frequently neglected command.)

But we should also praise the Lord because *He deserves our worship and praise.* He alone is worthy "to receive glory and honor and power" (Rev. 4:11). He is the God above all gods, the King above all kings, the Lord above all lords. There is no one like Him in heaven or on earth. He is worthy of all the praise we could ever lavish on Him.

We should praise the Lord because *God loves praise and He seeks worshipers* (John 4:23). Praise is important to God; every time you praise Him, you are fulfilling one of the deepest desires of His heart.

Similarly, we should praise the Lord because *we were made to bring Him pleasure—and* praise pleases Him. Do you ever wonder what your purpose is here on this earth? When you praise God, you are fulfilling the highest purpose for which He created you.

We should praise the Lord because *praise is the primary, eternal occupation of heaven.* In Revelation 4–5, God gives the apostle John a vision of the throne room of heaven. In that vision, John sees "four living creatures" who have one full-time responsibility, day and night: to worship the "Lord God, the Almighty" (4:8). They are joined by more than one hundred million angels who loudly proclaim the greatness and worth of the One who sits on that throne and the Lamb who was slain for our sin (5:11–13). The saints and citizens of heaven who have gone before us are there as well, praising and worshiping the Lord.

In a sense, then, when we praise the Lord here on earth, we are having a "dress rehearsal" for what we will spend an eternity doing in heaven. It's worth asking: How much "practice" are you and I getting in preparation for that eternal concert of praise in heaven?

But the value of praise is not just for the future. We should praise the Lord because *praise takes us into His presence and brings down His glory.* Psalm 22:3 (KJV) tells us that God inhabits the praises of His people. As I once heard a preacher put it, "Praise is God's address."

At the dedication of Solomon's temple, a massive choir sang, accompanied by 120 trumpeters as well as other instruments. First Chronicles 5:13–14 describes that unforgettable moment and its aftermath:

> When the song was raised ... in praise to the LORD,
> "For he is good,
> for his steadfast love endures forever,"
> the house, the house of the LORD, was filled with a cloud
> ... for the glory of the LORD filled the house of God."

Do you want to see the glory of God? Do you want to be close to Him? Then accept the psalmist's invitation to

> enter his gates with thanksgiving,
> and his courts with praise. (Ps. 100:4)

That praise will take you right up to His throne and into the place of His most intimate presence.

Yet another reason we should praise the Lord is that *praise*

THE PERFUME OF PRAISE

is an antidote for spiritual dryness. God has created us in such a way that we are thirsty for Him. When we look to things and people on this earth to satisfy our thirst, our souls become parched and discontent. But when we lift our eyes up to Him in praise, our hearts are filled.

One day when David was hiding out from King Saul in the wilderness of Judah, painfully conscious of the dryness and neediness in his soul, he discovered this powerful secret:

> You, God, are my God,
>   earnestly I seek you;
> I thirst for you,
>   my whole being longs for you,
> in a dry and parched land
>   where there is no water.
>
> I have seen you in the sanctuary
>   and beheld your power and your glory.
> Because your love is better than life,
>   my lips will glorify you.
> I will praise you as long as I live,
>   and in your name I will lift up my hands.
> I will be fully satisfied as with the richest of foods;
>   with singing lips my mouth will praise you. (Ps. 63:1–5)

Are you spiritually dry and thirsty? Begin to praise the Lord and He will fill you with Himself until your thirst is quenched and your cup overflows.

Another important reason to praise the Lord is that *praise defeats Satan*. Satan hates praise because Satan hates God and anything that exalts or pleases God. And one of his favorite strategies is to get us to focus on ourselves—our needs, our problems, our circumstances, our feelings—instead of on the One who loves us best. But when we lift our eyes up, though they may be filled with tears, and choose to praise the Lord, Satan's plan is defeated and God is victorious in our lives.

When Satan tempted Jesus to fall down and worship him, Jesus responded by quoting Scripture:

> You shall worship the Lord your God
> and him only . . .

And the moment that Jesus expressed His commitment to worship God alone, "the devil left him, and behold, angels came and were ministering to him" (Matt. 4:10–11).

Has Satan tormented you with fears and doubts? Do you find yourself being bombarded with temptation to sin? Try praising the Lord, and watch Satan flee.

Finally, we should praise the Lord because *praise sets us free from spiritual bondage*. Ask Jonah. Sitting in the belly of that great fish, he began to cry out to the Lord, first in humility, then in worship. And the minute the repenting prophet spoke words of praise, "I with a song of thanksgiving will sacrifice to you" (Jonah 2:9), he was delivered from his fishy prison. "The LORD spoke to the fish, and it vomited Jonah out onto dry land (v. 10).

Praise precedes and prepares for deliverance. Ask Paul and Silas. In the middle of the night, prisoners in a Roman dungeon in Philippi, they turned their focus away from their wounds and looked heavenward with hymns of praise. God was so pleased that He sent a little heavenly accompaniment in the form of an earthquake that shook the foundations of the prison and caused the prison doors to fling wide open (Acts 16:16–34).

Are you living in some kind of prison? Perhaps you are in bondage to your past, to painful memories, to past failures, to the expectations of others, or to some sinful habit that enslaves you. Your prison may be the consequence of your own disobedience, as it was with Jonah. Or it may result from others' wrongdoing, as in the case of Paul and Silas. If you've sinned, repentance is of course your first step. But then lift up your heart from your prison cell, start to praise the Lord, and watch God begin to open the prison doors. Your circumstances may or may not change, but *you* will change. Your heart will be released. God will set you free.

A LIFESTYLE OF PRAISE

Praise, worship, and thanksgiving are to be the eternal occupation of every believer. And praise is not just an activity we do at scheduled times; it is to be *a continuous lifestyle.*

> Praise is not just an activity we do at scheduled times; it is to be a continuous lifestyle.

We have seen that the Old Testament priests offered up "perpetual incense" to God every morning and every evening (Ex. 30:7–8 NKJV), symbolizing the prayers and praise of God's people ascending to His throne. This incense was burned at the same time the oil lamps were lit, implying that each time the lamp of God's Word is lit in our hearts, we are also to offer up prayers and praise to Him.

The importance of continual praise is a recurring theme throughout both the Old and New Testaments:

> It is good to give thanks to the LORD,
>   to sing praises to your name, O Most High;
> to declare your steadfast love in the morning,
>   and your faithfulness by night. (Ps. 92:1–2)

> I will bless the LORD at all times;
> his praise shall continually be in my mouth. (Ps. 34:1)
>
> Every day will I bless you
> and praise your name forever and ever. (Ps. 145:2)
>
> By [Jesus] therefore let us continually offer up a sacrifice of praise to God, that is, the fruit of lips that acknowledge his name. (Heb. 13:15)

If we're honest, though, it's not easy to offer up praise continually. Sometimes we're down or distracted or downright depressed, and praise is the last thing we feel like doing. But praise, according to Scripture, is *an expression of faith and an act of the will.* It is not based on how we feel.

David understood this concept well. In Psalm 34, we find him in one of the darkest periods of his life. Years earlier he had received God's promise that he was to be the next king, but the insecure egomaniac who occupied the throne (Saul) was determined to take his life. So David found himself fleeing for his life, living as a fugitive in the wilderness. All the ingredients were there to set him up for a major depression. But instead he made a choice—a choice to praise the Lord regardless of his natural feelings:

> I *will* bless the Lord at all times;
> his praise shall continually be in my mouth. (Ps. 34:1)

When he determined to focus on the Lord instead of his circumstances, David's heart was lifted, as were the hearts of others around him:

> My soul makes its boast in the LORD;
> let the humble ["the afflicted," NIV] hear and be glad.

THE PERFUME OF PRAISE

> Oh, magnify the LORD with me,
> and let us exalt his name together! (Ps. 34:2–3)

Praise is not meant to be a response to our circumstances, which constantly fluctuate. Praise is a response to the goodness and love of a God who never changes. That is why David could say,

> My heart is steadfast, O God,
> my heart is steadfast;
> I will sing, yes, I will sing praises! (Ps. 57:7 NASB)

It didn't matter to David whether he was sitting on the throne or being pursued by the one who was. It didn't matter whether he was hungry or full, happy or sad, alone or with friends. All that mattered was that God was there. And as long as God was there he could choose to praise.

Praise demonstrates faith that God is bigger and greater than any circumstance we may be facing. And faith pleases God—that is why He loves it when we choose to praise Him, regardless of how we feel.

Praise is *a ministry to God*. It is first and foremost for God, not for us. The purpose of praise is to bring *Him* blessing and pleasure, not to make *us* feel good. In our narcissistic, sensual culture, "praise and worship" has become for many believers a "spiritual," even erotic, expression of self-love—a means of experiencing self-fulfillment. This is far from true worship and is not pleasing to the Lord.

In Exodus 30, God gave Moses the precise "recipe" for making the incense that was to be used in the temple worship. Then He emphasized:

It shall be most holy for you. And the incense that you shall make according to its composition, you shall not make for yourselves. It shall be for you holy to the Lord. Whoever makes any like it to use as perfume shall be cut off from his people.
(Ex. 30:36–38)

The same can be said of worship. Though it will bring about many benefits and blessings in our lives, its ultimate purpose is to bless the Lord, not to satisfy us.

Praise is to be both public and private, much as a husband and wife may display their affection for each other both in the company of others as well as when they are alone.

Many Scriptures speak of praising the Lord in the company of His people:

> Let them extol him in the congregation of the people,
> and praise him in the assembly of the elders.
> (Ps. 107:32)

> With my mouth I will give great praise to the Lord;
> I will praise him in the midst of the throng.
> (Ps. 109:30)

> I will give thanks to the Lord with my whole heart,
> in the company of the upright, in the congregation.
> (Ps. 111:1)

At other times, however, praise is a private expression of love between us and our Beloved. For example, though Daniel in the Old Testament was a busy, high-ranking government official, "Three times a day he got down on his knees and prayed, giving thanks to his God" (Dan. 6:10). In much the same way, the psalmist said,

> Seven times a day I praise you
>   for your righteous rules. (Ps. 119:164)

Whether public or private, however, praise requires personal participation—it is not a spectator sport. There's no shortage of Christian artists, recordings, and concerts today. And while these can be a blessing, they also have contributed to a spectator mindset when it comes to praise and worship. Like the world around us, the Christian world has developed an addiction to being entertained. Just turn down the houselights, shine some spotlights on the stage, and let us sit back and enjoy the performance. At home or in the car, many believers who love listening to others sing songs of praise may be hesitant to lift up their own voices to the Lord (especially when they compare their voice to the "professionals" they hear onstage or on their devices).

But if there's one group of people in the world who ought to love to sing, it's those who have been redeemed, for they are the ones who truly have something to sing about. According to the apostle Paul, the singing of "psalms and hymns and spiritual songs" is an unmistakable evidence of being filled with the Spirit and of having a grateful heart (Eph. 5:19; Col. 3:16).

The psalms of David represent one man's intensely personal response to what God had revealed to him about His heart and His ways. They are not a collection of someone else's songs that the psalmist merely listened to; they are songs he wrote and sang from his own heart to the Lord. Throughout the Psalms there's a sense of David entering into worship with all his heart:

> Bless the LORD, O my soul,
>   and all that is within me,
>   bless his holy name. (Ps. 103:1)

> I give you thanks, O Lord, with my whole heart;
> before the gods I sing your praise.
> I bow down toward your holy temple
> and give thanks to your name for your steadfast
> love and your faithfulness. (Ps. 138:1–2)

Many years ago, while spending the night in the home of a friend, I had an unforgettable experience. A Nigerian pastor and his wife were also guests in the same home that night. In the middle of the night, I was awakened by a sound unlike anything I had heard before. In the bedroom next to mine, that dear couple was singing "How Great Thou Art"—slowly, loudly, with a heavy accent, and with all their hearts. I wasn't sure I hadn't died and gone to heaven!

That man and woman were not spectators. They were active participants in the great eternal concert of praise, singing for a sacred audience of One.

> O that with yonder sacred throng
> We at His feet may fall!
> We'll join the everlasting song,
> And crown Him Lord of all![2]

QUIET-TIME PRAISE

So how do we worship the Lord in our daily time alone with Him? Remember that worship, praise, and thanksgiving are a response to God's revelation of Himself. As He shows Himself to you and speaks to you through His Word, you'll find yourself wanting to respond to Him in praise—*verbal* or *visible* adoration of God for who He is and what He has done.

True praise is more than just mental appreciation; it involves outward expression. Over and over (as many as seventy-five times), the Psalms refer to praising the Lord, and the word translated "praise" is the Hebrew verb *halal*, which means "to be clear . . . to shine; hence, to make a show, to boast; and thus to be (clamorously) foolish; to rave; causatively, to celebrate."[3] There's nothing quiet or reserved about any of those definitions!

That's not to say that our outward expressions of praise need to be raucous or unrestrained. It doesn't even mean that we can't sometimes praise God quietly in our heart, without saying a word. But even when we're alone with God, there's no reason why we can't express your worship with everything we have—body, soul, spirit, and voice. Our praise can be written, as we saw in the last chapter. It can be spoken or sung out loud. It can be expressed physically through various postures and forms of movement.

Many different expressions of praise and worship are taught and illustrated in the Scripture. Ask the Holy Spirit to direct you in your times of personal worship, and follow His lead. Here are some of the ways He may lead you to respond.

Use Different Physical Positions

Kneeling or bowing before the Lord is a position I have often found myself taking in my personal worship. This is a position that is frequently referred to in the Scripture:

> Oh come, let us worship and bow down;
>   let us kneel before the Lord, our Maker! (Ps. 95:6)

> When all the people of Israel saw the fire come down and the glory of the Lord on the temple, they bowed down with their faces to the ground on the pavement and worshiped and gave thanks to the Lord, saying, "For he is good, for his steadfast love endures forever. (2 Chron. 7:3)

Twenty-nine times in the Psalms, when we read the phrase "bless the Lord," the Hebrew word *barak* is used in the original text, a word that means "to kneel"; by implication, "to bless God (as an act of adoration)."[4]

Have you taken time to bless the Lord today? Regardless of what is going on in your life at this moment, God is good; He is worthy of your praise. Before reading any further, why not pause and take a few moments to kneel before the Lord? Bless Him, adore Him, worship Him.

Sometimes you may wish to *stand* before the Lord, as the Israelites did during the great revival in Nehemiah's day (Neh. 9) and at the dedication of the temple (2 Chron. 7:5–6). Hymn writer James Montgomery urges us to

> Stand up and bless the Lord,
>   Ye people of His choice;
> Stand up and bless the Lord your God
>   With heart and soul and voice.[5]

At other times, your awareness of the holiness and greatness of God may move you to *fall prostrate on your face* before the Lord. John's vision in Revelation records that the twenty-four elders who surround the throne of God "fall down before him who is seated on the throne and worship him who lives forever and ever" (Rev. 4:10).

The Scripture speaks of another physical expression of worship that involves the use of our hands. Psalm 47:1 tells us to *clap our hands* in praise to the Lord. The idea behind clapping our hands is not just to keep time or add rhythm to our singing. Nor is the purpose of clapping to generate a more exuberant atmosphere.

When I think of clapping to the Lord, I think of a small

child who claps with glee as she steps into the waves lapping the beach or as she opens a brightly wrapped box under the Christmas tree and is delighted to discover the doll she has been longing for. I think of the applause of an adoring throng when the king comes out on the balcony and warmly greets his subjects.

Clapping to the Lord is the spontaneous, glad response of the sons and daughters of God when they step into the river of His delights or have just discovered a gift of His grace. It is the joyful, heartfelt response of the subjects of King Jesus when He steps into their midst and touches their lives with His presence and His love.

Not only can we use our hands to clap to the Lord, but Psalm 134:2 speaks of *lifting our hands* to the Lord. Some fifty times in the Psalms, the words *thank* or *praise* are used to translate a Hebrew word (*yadah*) that means "to revere or worship (with extended hands)."[6]

The lifting of hands to the Lord is an expression of worship meant to signify that God is high and lifted up, that we are infinitely beneath Him, that we are dependent upon Him, and that we acknowledge His right to rule over us. Hands lifted up to the Lord say, "I surrender all, Your Majesty."

Of course, no physical position is inherently more worshipful than another. This visible expression of worship is merely intended to express—or help cultivate within us—a heart attitude of surrender and reverence.

Open Your Mouth and Speak

Have you ever noticed how often Scripture instructs us to use our mouths to express praise and thanksgiving and to declare the greatness of God?

> I will speak of your splendor and glorious majesty
> and your wondrous works....
> My mouth will declare the Lord's praise. (Ps. 145:5, 21 CSB)
>
> I will bless the Lord at all times;
> his praise shall continually be in my mouth. (Ps. 34:1)
>
> Let us continually offer up a sacrifice of praise to God, that is, the fruit of lips that acknowledge his name. (Heb. 13:15)

You might wonder why speaking praise aloud is important. Is it better than, say, speaking it in your head—especially when you're alone? What benefits does speaking aloud bring? I don't know all the answers to those questions. But I know that Scripture emphasizes the power of the tongue (see Prov. 18:21). Verbal praise expresses and strengthens faith as we align our words and our emotions with His truth. Speaking aloud engages more senses than just internal thought and deepens our confidence in the truth. It helps to focus and rein in wandering thoughts. And declaring the truth can be a weapon against the evil one and the powers of darkness (see Ps. 8:2; Rev. 12:11).

Frequently, as I am reading a passage of Scripture that reveals to me something of the heart and ways of God or the beauty of the Lord Jesus, I pause to respond by blessing the Lord aloud, affirming what I have just read.

Sometimes I bless Him with my mouth by reading aloud portions of the Psalms or other Scripture passages that are directed to Him. Sometimes I will read poems or song lyrics or simply voice my own words of praise to Him. These are ways, as the hymn puts it, to "tell out, my soul, the great greatness of the Lord."[7]

Having voiced our praise to the Lord, it follows that we will want to speak of Him to others. Hardly a day goes by that you and I do not have one or more such opportunities to declare His goodness, grace, and wonderful works, whether to brothers and sisters in Christ or to those who know little or nothing about Him. In so doing, we join the witness of creation and Scripture in exalting His name throughout the earth.

A variation on speaking to (and about) the Lord is *shouting to the Lord*. It's not that God is hard of hearing, but sometimes our joy in Him simply calls for loud exclamations. Psalm 32:11 (NASB) tells us to "shout for joy, all you who are upright in heart." The Hebrew word that is translated "shout" in that verse is a word that means "to creak; to shout for joy."[8] (Numerous times in the Psalms, the same Hebrew word is translated "sing," as in Psalm 30:4.) A different word is used in Psalm 47:1, translated in the NKJV as "shout to God with the voice of triumph." This word means "to split the ears with sound."[9] If you, like me, are more introverted and rarely raise your voice about anything, this idea may seem strange or uncomfortable. But there are occasions when it is fitting to get past our natural inhibitions (or perhaps pride?) and express our praise in an unfettered way.

Sing to the Lord

This is one of my favorite expressions of praise, and one that I believe merits special attention beyond what has already been said in this chapter. In the Psalms alone, there are sixty-eight references to singing to the Lord. We are told to sing praises to the Lord; to sing aloud about His righteousness, His power, and His mercy; to sing forth the honor of His name; to sing for joy; to sing of mercy and judgment; to sing a new song unto the Lord; to sing psalms unto Him; to sing the Lord's song in a strange land; and to sing aloud upon our beds.

Next to meditating on Scripture itself, singing—both to and about the Lord—has probably been the activity that has produced the greatest encouragement, blessing, and joy in my Christian walk. My relationship with the Lord has been deepened and enriched by singing biblically grounded hymns and spiritual songs, many of which have been sung by past generations of saints and which I first learned as a child.

But I'm not a singer, you may object. Let me assure you, I get that. To my recollection, I have never once been asked to sing in a music group or public setting. My mother had a gorgeous, trained, operatic voice. My dad, by contrast, could barely carry a tune and did not have a voice anyone would recruit for a choir or worship team. I clearly have his genes on that front. However, my dad's lack of musical giftedness did not keep him from singing to the Lord. I can still hear him standing during the music portion of church services, surrounded by his seven children and his musically talented wife, singing out to the Lord—"lustily," as Methodist founder, John Wesley, encouraged God's people to do in his "Directions for Singing."[10]

> As we sing, we express faith that what we are singing is true; we counsel our own hearts; we are transformed as we turn our eyes upon Jesus.

Singing to the Lord is not for some select few voices; it is for me and it is for you. It is not simply a religious exercise or an emotional outlet. As we sing, we express faith that what we are singing is true; we counsel our own hearts; we are transformed as we turn our eyes upon Jesus; and we declare His faithfulness and His redeeming love to one another.

Singing to the Lord is also a powerful weapon in overcoming

THE PERFUME OF PRAISE

the enemy. Before he exalted himself against God and was cast out of heaven, Lucifer may have had a major role in leading the music and worship of heaven. Some Bible versions translate Ezekiel 28:13, which is probably addressed to the fallen angel, as referring to musical instruments:

> the workmanship of your timbrels and pipes
> was prepared for you on the day you were created.
> (Ezek. 28:13 NKJV)

Whatever his role before the fall, Satan certainly knows the power of music as a means of praise. He knows how much God loves to hear the musical worship of His creatures. He knows the power of praise to deliver us from bondage. So he strives to keep us from singing or tempts us to make music for our own pleasure and gratification rather than to magnify and exalt the Lord.

Over and over again, I have seen the power of singing praise to defeat Satan and to overcome emotional bondage that he may have led us into. Discouragement, fear, anxiety, depression, grief—in many cases, these will flee as we sing to the Lord. On occasion, I have felt as if an enormous dark cloud were hanging over my spirit. Invariably, as I have sung to the Lord—sometimes through tears and with a trembling voice—the cloud has lifted and the sunlight of His sweet peace and grace has poured in, quickening and encouraging my heart.

Some years ago I had the unforgettable experience of participating in the weekly Tuesday evening prayer meeting at the Brooklyn Tabernacle in New York City. I arrived several minutes after the service had already begun to find the auditorium packed with wall-to-wall people. The gathering was diverse—old and young, professionals and blue-collar workers, well dressed and poorly dressed, many races and ethnicities—all praising and praying together side by side.

One of the things that particularly touched me that night was the singing. It was so earnest and full that at times it sounded like peals of thunder or a freight train moving through the room. It has been a long time since I have heard such uninhibited, heartfelt singing. I was reminded of that occasion during the great revival in Nehemiah's day when "the singers sang loudly . . . so that the joy of Jerusalem was heard afar off" (Neh. 12:42–43 NKJV).

When I learned something of the people who were in the audience that night, I understood better why they sang as they did. Many of the men and women in that church had come to Christ from backgrounds of drug addiction, alcoholism, violent crime, and sexual promiscuity. They knew what it was to be enslaved to sin. They knew what it was to be without hope and without Christ. And they knew what it was to have God reach down and rescue them by His grace. They knew what it was to be redeemed by the blood of the Lamb. They had not forgotten where God found them.

When those men and women sang about the love and the mercy and the greatness of God, they knew what they were singing about. They sang like they meant it—because they did.

And the sweet perfume of their praise filled every corner of that space.

> Praise, my soul, the King of heaven,
> To His feet thy tribute bring;
> Ransomed, healed, restored, forgiven,
> Evermore His praises sing;
> Alleluia! Alleluia!
> Praise the everlasting King.[11]

MAKE IT PERSONAL

1. Of the various expressions of praise referred to in this chapter, which ones are you most accustomed to? Which ones are you least comfortable with? Why?

2. What are some of the obstacles you have experienced that have made it difficult to praise the Lord with all your heart?

What have you learned in this chapter that has motivated you to cultivate a lifestyle of praise and worship?

3. Read Psalm 145 aloud.
    - What does this passage reveal about what God is like and what He has done? Make a list.

    - Pray this psalm back to God, personalizing it and praising Him for each of His attributes and blessings (for example, in verse 8: "Lord, I praise You for the grace and compassion that You have poured out on me. You have given me so much more than I deserve; Your love toward me is greater than any other love I have ever known...").

4. Write your own psalm of praise, thanking God for His character, for His works on your behalf, and for physical and spiritual blessings you have received from Him. Say or sing it out loud.

5. Sing a psalm or hymn to the Lord each day for the next week. You may want to sing along with an online video or a music streaming app. Or try singing out of a hymnal, making up a tune for one of your favorite psalms, or even composing your own lyrics and singing them to the Lord.

CHAPTER 11

The Privilege of Prayer

My most important appointment today is with Jesus in prayer.

For many years, as I settled into my quiet-time chair to meet with the Lord each morning, I saw those words on a plaque given to me by a praying friend. I needed that reminder back then—and still do—because my mind so easily drifts off to other "important" appointments and tasks that lie ahead.

The truth is, all too often I find myself in a hurry to get through my devotions so I can move on to the other demands and business of the day. But the words on that plaque have often pressed me to pause and take stock and to face God's perspective of what really matters. I, too, need to hear what Jesus said to that first-century homemaker who was harried and uptight about getting her to-do list all checked off:

> "Martha, Martha, you are worried and bothered about so many things; but *only one* thing is necessary,

for Mary has chosen the good part, which shall not be taken away from her." (LUKE 10:41–42 NASB)

This chapter has been the most difficult one of this book for me to write. I have always loved to read, study, memorize, and meditate on the Word. But prayer has never come easily for me.

I don't want to speak on this or any subject beyond the reality of my life. At the same time, I want to convince you of what I know in my heart to be true—that prayer matters and that rich communion with God in prayer can be a daily reality and practice in each of our lives.

PRAYERLESSNESS

A number of years ago the Lord began to speak to me about my prayerlessness. It's not that I *never* prayed—I tried to live each day in a spirit of prayer, seeking to know the heart and mind of God in relation to my activities and relationships and to know what would please Him in each decision and circumstance. But with few exceptions over the years, I had never cultivated a practice of set times for private prayer. Others may have assumed that I was a woman of prayer, but God knew and I knew that was not the case.

I'd like to say that what followed was a major breakthrough that resulted in my becoming the prayer warrior I wanted to be. In my case, there has been no such breakthrough. However, what God began in my heart that summer led to an ongoing process and a commitment to press on, to lay hold of the heart and hand of God through prayer.

As God opened my eyes to this matter of prayerlessness, I asked Him to let me see it from His point of view. Here is what I wrote in my journal in that season:

I am convicted that prayerlessness ...

___ is a sin against God: "Far be it from me that I should sin against the Lord by ceasing to pray for you." (1 Sam. 12:23)

___ is direct disobedience to the command of Christ: "Watch and pray." (Matt. 26:41); and to the Word of God: "Pray without ceasing." (1 Thess. 5:17)

___ makes me vulnerable to temptation: "Watch and pray that you may not enter into temptation." (Matt. 26:41)

___ expresses independence—no need for God

___ gives place to the enemy and makes me vulnerable to his schemes (Eph. 6:10–20)

___ results in powerlessness

___ limits (and defines) my relationship with God

___ hinders me from knowing His will, His priorities, His direction

___ forces me to operate in the realm of the natural (what I can do) versus the supernatural (what He can do)

___ leaves me weak, harried, and hassled

___ is rooted in pride, self-sufficiency, laziness, and lack of discipline

___ reveals a lack of real burden and compassion for others

WHY WE DON'T PRAY

Since that time, I have pondered the question: Why don't we pray more? Why don't *I* pray more? Here's one reason I particularly relate to—maybe you do as well:

We don't pray because we're not desperate. We're not really conscious of our *need* for God. Puritan pastor William Gurnall makes this point in his writings:

> Perhaps the deadness of thy heart in prayer ariseth from not having a deep sense of thy wants, and the mercies thou art in need of.... The hungry man needs no help to teach him how to beg.[1]

In the last chapter I mentioned visiting the Brooklyn Tabernacle, a church that is known as a praying church. During that visit Pastor Jim Cymbala explained to us why it's not hard for his people to pray:

> In our prayer meetings you've got *desperate people* crying out to God. Some of them don't have jobs. Others have husbands who are alcoholics or strung out on drugs. Many are women with no husband at all, trying to raise their children on welfare. Every day we are dealing with crack/cocaine addicts, people who have never had any family to speak of. These people are desperate! They *need* God; they don't have anywhere else to turn. That's why they pray.

In comparison to many of those who participate in the prayer meetings at the Brooklyn Tabernacle, my life has been relatively trouble free. I have never had to wonder where the next meal is coming from—so why would I be desperate to pray, "Give us this day our daily bread" (Matt. 6:11)? From a human standpoint I can live my life without God's help. I can operate, humanly speaking, on my own efforts, my own resources, apart from His grace and intervention.

I have a dear friend whose third child was born with multiple birth defects, including the lack of an esophagus. For years her son was in critical condition—in and out of hospitals, undergoing life-threatening surgeries, requiring a breathing apparatus every night, prone to choking, and frequently unable to breathe. Do you think anyone had to tell that mama to pray for her son? She knew her son's only hope of survival was for God to intervene and spare his life; she knew the only way she could get through those years of sleepless nights was for God to pour His grace into her life and grant supernatural strength and enabling. You couldn't keep her from praying! (In God's mercy, that much-prayed-for child is now married with children of his own and serving the Lord. He has no doubt that he owes his life to the One who heard and answered the prayers of a desperate mother.)

> *We can pray in seasons of ease and plenty. But if prayer is often birthed out of desperation, then anything that makes us conscious of our need for God is actually a blessing.*

Our natural instinct is to wish for a life free from pain, trouble, and adversity. Of course, we can pray in seasons of ease and plenty. But if prayer is often birthed out of desperation, then anything that makes us conscious of our need for God is actually a blessing.

HOW CAN I PRAY?

As I have moved toward God in prayer, here are several suggestions I have found helpful:

Ask the Lord Jesus to Teach You to Pray

When the disciples saw Jesus' prayer life, they were moved to appeal to Him, "Lord, teach *us* to pray." And He did. As I read the prayers of Jesus recorded in Scripture, I can't help but be touched by the intimate communion He shared with His heavenly Father. "Lord, please teach *me* to pray" has become my heart's desire.

Ask the Holy Spirit to Help You Pray

It's encouraging to me to know that someone as spiritually mature as the apostle Paul would confess, "We do not know how to pray as we should" (Rom. 8:26 NASB). He recognized his inability to pray according to God's will, apart from God's help. But he also recognized that God had made a provision for his need, that the Holy Spirit had been given as a Helper:

> The Spirit also helps us in our weakness; for we do not know how to pray as we should, but the Spirit Himself intercedes for us with groanings to deep for words; and He who searches the hearts knows what the mind of the Spirit is, because He intercedes for the saints according to the will of God. (Rom. 8:26–27 NASB)

At times, as you're praying for a particular individual or concern, you may need to say, "Holy Spirit, I don't know the will of the Father on this matter. I don't know how to pray. But the Word says that You will help me in my weakness, that You will intercede for me in accordance with the will of God. I ask You to do that now. I need You; please express to the Father what You know to be His will."

Pray the Word of God Back to God

We all know that we are to pray "according to the will of God." But how can we know His will? There are many matters on which it may be difficult to know the will of God. But we can be sure of one thing: the Word of God is the will of God. When we pray the Word of God back to God, we can be sure we are praying according to His will.

Two scriptural examples come to mind in this regard. The first is found in 2 Samuel 7, which records the occasion when David was seeking to know God's will regarding his desire to build a temple for God. In this case God revealed His will to David through the prophet Nathan. The word came back from God to David that he was not the one God had chosen to build a house for Him, but that David's son would be the one to build the house. Then God promised David that He would establish and bless him and his family and that David's family line would always include a king to sit on the throne: "Your house and your kingdom shall be made sure forever before me. Your throne shall be established forever" (2 Sam. 7:16).

Verses 18–29 record the prayer that David prayed in response to the words God had spoken to him. He began by expressing wonder and gratitude that God would deal so graciously with His servant. He praised God: "You are great, O LORD God! For there is none like you, and there is no God besides you" (2 Sam. 7:22). Then he went on to make his petition to the Lord. His whole petition was based on what God had already promised him:

> And now, O LORD God, confirm forever the word that you have spoken concerning your servant and concerning his house, and do as you have spoken. And your name will be magnified forever, saying, "The LORD of hosts is God over Israel!"...
>
> For you, O LORD of hosts, the God of Israel, have made this revelation to your servant, saying, "I will build you a house." Therefore your servant has found courage to pray this prayer to you. And now, O LORD God, you are God, and your words are true, and you have promised this good thing to your servant. Now therefore may it please you to bless the house of your servant, so that it may continue forever before you. For you, O LORD God, have spoken. (2 Sam. 7:25–29)

What was David saying in those verses? In a nutshell: "Lord, I'm asking You to do what You have already promised to do. I dare to ask boldly because You have told me this is Your will."

Daniel was another man who knew how to pray according to God's Word. Daniel 9:2–3 illustrates:

> I, Daniel, understood from the Scriptures, according to the word of the LORD given to Jeremiah the prophet, that the desolation of Jerusalem would last seventy years. *So I turned to the Lord God and pleaded with him in prayer and petition,* in fasting, and in sackcloth and ashes. (NIV)

How did Daniel know what to pray in this instance? He had he read Jeremiah's prophecy that said the Jewish nation would be in exile for seventy years. So he began to pray that God would deliver His people from captivity.

Knowing the outcome (that the captivity would last for seventy years) did not cause Daniel to sit back and wait for it to happen. Rather, knowing the will of God motivated him to pray more fervently:

> For your sake, Lord, look with favor on your desolate sanctuary. Give ear, our God, and hear; open your eyes and see the desolation of the city that bears your Name. . . . Lord, listen! Lord, forgive! Lord, hear and act! For your sake, my God, do not delay. (Dan. 9:17–19 NIV)

Daniel prayed according to the Scriptures he had read. He prayed for God's will—as it had already been revealed—to be done on earth. In his prayer Daniel aligned himself with the heart, the plan, and the purposes of God. Through prayer he became a partner with God in the fulfilling of those purposes.

There's nothing wrong with letting the Lord know the desires and requests that are on our hearts. In fact, He tells us to "pray about everything" (Phil. 4:6 TLB). But when we lay hold of His will as He has expressed it in His Word, we can pray boldly, with confidence that He not only hears, but He will grant those things we have asked of Him (1 John 5:14–15).

For example, I have a number of friends whose marriages are struggling. I often feel at a loss as to exactly how to pray for them. But I know I can pray confidently when I pray according to God's will as it is revealed in His Word. I know it is God's will for these husbands to love their wife in the selfless, sacrificing, serving way that Jesus loves His church (Eph. 5:25). I know it is God's will for them to dwell with their wives in an understanding way and to honor them

(1 Peter 3:7). I know it is God's will for these wives to respect their husbands and to submit to him as to the Lord (Eph. 5:22–33). I know it is God's will that these couples walk in love, oneness, and truth. So I pray these and other passages for them, calling upon God's revealed will to be fulfilled in their lives and marriages.

When we have unmet needs or desires or are lacking direction, Scripture urges us to make our requests known to the Lord. While we cannot demand that He will do as we desire, we can boldly ask Him for anything He has revealed to be His will in His Word: that He will direct our steps, that He will protect us from selfish desires or from anything that might be harmful to our walk with Him, that He will grant us wisdom as we make decisions, and that we will have a contented and grateful heart, whether or not He chooses to provide exactly what we have desired or thought we needed.

WHAT SHOULD WE PRAY FOR?

Many people find it helpful to use some sort of prayer list to organize their prayer life. Others feel that such lists tend to make their praying more mechanical and perfunctory. Regardless of whether you choose to use a prayer list, there are several categories of need that we ought to pray for on a regular basis.

Pray for the Advancement of Christ's Kingdom in the World

The first three petitions of the Lord's Prayer focus on this concern.

"Hallowed be your name" (Matt. 6:9). Your Name is holy.

May Your Name be worshiped and honored by Your people everywhere. May our lives in no way bring disrespect or dishonor to Your great Name. And may all peoples of the earth come to revere Your sacred Name.

"*Your kingdom come*" *(v. 10).*

> Your kingdom is an everlasting kingdom, and your dominion endures throughout all generations. (Ps. 145:13)
>
> May [you] have dominion from sea to sea." (Ps. 72:8)

May Your kingdom be established throughout this entire world. May You rule and reign supreme this day in my heart and in the hearts of Your people. And hasten the day when "the kingdom of the world [will] become the kingdom of our Lord . . . and [you will] reign forever and ever" (Rev. 11:15).

"*Your will be done on earth as it is in heaven*" *(v. 10).* May You have Your way this day in my life and in the lives of Your people throughout the earth. May we live in submission to You, even as the hosts of heaven seek only to know and to do Your will (Ps. 103:21). Fulfill all Your holy purposes in the nations and peoples of the earth this day.

In offering up these petitions to God, we are making His priorities our priorities. We are saying that what matters most to Him matters most to us. We are subordinating our own personal needs and agenda to the wider concerns of His kingdom.

Pray for Others

In my case, those others include my husband and family members, friends, the staff of the ministry in which I serve, pastors and Christian leaders, our president and other elected officials, and non-Christian neighbors and friends. In recent years I have been using a daily prayer journal to record prayers for specific people who are on my mind.

As I pray for others, I sometimes feel prompted to stop and send a text or jot a note to individuals that I sense need special encouragement. I may express appreciation for their life or ministry, or share a Scripture that is on my heart for them, or just let them know what the Lord has put on my heart to pray for them.

Saturday night and Sunday morning are a good time to intercede for pastors who are serving the Lord and preaching His Word in our own local churches, throughout the country, and around the world. Pray that they will be freshly anointed by God's Spirit, that their hearts and motives will be pure, that they will not fear other people but will fear only the Lord, that they will boldly proclaim the truth of His Word, that God will encourage them in their ministry, and that those who listen to them preach will tremble at the Word of the Lord and will have ears to hear and hearts to respond to what God says.

God has been gracious to raise up around me an incredible team of "praying friends." Many of those individuals, some of whom do not know me well, have shared that they pray for me *every single day*. I cannot imagine what blessing and protection I would be missing if it were not for their faithful, fervent prayers on my behalf. The impact of their prayers on my life inspires me to intercede on behalf of those that God has put on my heart.

I don't think we can fully fathom the effect our prayers can have on the lives of others. As Andrew Bonar points out: "How much we may be to blame for the faults of others not being cured! We point to their faults and failings, but we don't pray for them."[2]

Let me say a special word of encouragement to mothers or grandmothers who are carrying a burden for your children or grandchildren—especially those who may be far from the Lord. You may sometimes cry yourself to sleep at night over their condition. You may be at your wit's end and feel you have nowhere to turn for help. But whatever you do, don't stop praying.

In a sense, I believe my life is the product of a praying great-grandmother. I never met *Yaya*, my father's Greek immigrant grandmother, but I know that she was a praying woman. After coming to America, Yaya lived in a house in upstate New York with her two sons, two daughters-in-law (who were sisters), and four grandsons. One of those grandchildren, my dad's first cousin, Ted DeMoss, shared a bedroom with Yaya when he was a little boy. Before he went to heaven, I recall hearing Ted tell of nights when Yaya would be on her knees praying in her native tongue as he went to sleep. She was praying for the salvation of her children and grandchildren. On some mornings, Ted told us, he would awaken to find Yaya still on her knees, praying for her family.

Eventually all four of Yaya's grandsons came to faith in Christ. I believe my father's dramatic conversion in 1950 was an answer to her prayers. Likewise, I believe that the scores of Yaya's great-grandchildren and great-great-grandchildren (and in the generation beyond) who are walking with the Lord today are the fruit of her faithful prayers.

You may have no idea when or how God will answer your prayers—sometimes it takes years or even decades—but *don't stop praying*. Andrew Bonar gives this word of encouragement when the answer to our prayers is delayed: "The blessing we pray for may not come at once, but it is on its way. Sometimes the Lord keeps us waiting long, because He likes to keep us in His presence."[3]

Pray for Yourself

"But isn't that selfish?" you may wonder. Not if your motivation is for God to be glorified through your life. On a day-to-day basis, I lay various personal matters before the Lord. I seek His direction in relation to my schedule, my priorities, my relationships, my work, and my physical and spiritual needs. As I pray about an issue, I try to listen to the Lord and be sensitive to how He may be directing my mind in relation to it.

On a recent morning, for example, as I was praying for direction on a specific issue, I felt impressed to call a particular individual to ask for prayer and input. I believe the Lord brought that person's name to mind as I was in prayer and then used that friend's prayerful counsel to help direct my steps.

There are several personal petitions I make to the Lord more often than most others. Through the years, these are requests I have made over and over again. (Since these are all Scripture-based, I know I am praying according to God's will.)

- *Guard my heart.* Make and keep it pure. Guard my motives, my attitudes, my values, and my responses to the circumstances of life. Protect me from the schemes and attacks of the evil one.

- *Fill me with Your love.* Help me love You with all my heart, soul, mind, and strength. Make me compassionate and sensitive to the needs of others around me. Help me give of myself to meet the needs of others without expecting anything in return.

- *Fill me with Your Spirit.* May I be emptied of myself and filled with Jesus. May my life be lived in the realm of the supernatural. Anoint my life and ministry with supernatural power.

- *Clothe me in humility.* May I be broken—poor in spirit—toward You and toward others. May I esteem all others as better than myself. May I not seek to impress others or to gain their praise, but instead seek only to please You.

- *Make me a servant.* Help me to serve You with gladness, to render each act of service as unto Christ, to joyously accept even "menial" or "unfulfilling" responsibilities. Help me to serve heartily, happily, humbly.

- *Guard my tongue.* "Set a guard, O Lord, over my mouth; keep watch over the door of my lips" (Ps. 141:3). May I speak only words that are true, words that help and heal, words that are wise and kind (Prov. 31:26).

- *Give me wisdom and discernment.* Help me to see all of life from Your point of view. May my life be ruled by the wisdom of Your Word. Give me the "wisdom that is from above . . . pure, then peaceable, gentle, open to reason, full of mercy and good fruits, impartial and sincere" (James 3:17).

- *Give me a grateful spirit and a thankful heart.* Help me give thanks in everything. Help me acknowledge and express the benefits and blessings that I have received from You and others. Protect me from a discontented heart and a murmuring tongue.

- *Help me to walk by faith and not by sight.* May my life show the world how great, how good, and how powerful You are. May I be willing to step out in faith when I cannot see the outcome, and may my life not be explainable in human terms.

- *Teach me the fear of the Lord.* Help me to practice the conscious, constant awareness that You see, hear, and know all. Help me live my life in light of the final judgment and as one who will give account to You.

"What Is Your Request? . . . It Shall Be Given You."

In the Old Testament book of Esther we find a scene that provides meaningful insight on prayer.

Totally apart from any initiative or effort on her part, God sovereignly arranged for Esther to be placed in a position of great influence at a crucial moment in Israel's history. Esther couldn't see the script God had written in heaven and was carrying out on earth. The entire Jewish nation stood in the balance, as wicked Haman set out to destroy the chosen people of God. For a brief time, from earth's vantage point, it seemed he was going to succeed. (When you look around and it appears that the enemy has God in a checkmate position, don't despair. Remember, we see things from a limited, finite point of view. God is still on His throne, and His purposes will not be thwarted.)

You may know the story—if not, it's a great read! When Mordecai, Esther's cousin and the object of Haman's hatred, discovered the insidious plot to annihilate the Jews, he immediately appealed to Queen Esther to exercise her royal position by interceding before King Artaxerxes on behalf of her people.

Esther's initial hesitation stemmed from one important fact. She knew that no one dared approach the king without being invited—not even the queen. For her to initiate an audience with him was to risk death—unless he chose to have mercy and extend his golden scepter in welcome.

Mordecai finally persuaded Esther that she had been placed in her current position for a purpose greater than herself and that she simply must get involved. After three days of fasting, Esther put on her royal robes and entered the inner court of the palace where the king sat on his throne. I love those next two verses:

> And when the king saw Queen Esther standing in the court, *she won favor in his sight*, and he held out to Esther the golden scepter that was in his hand. Then Esther approached and touched the tip of the scepter. And the king said to her, "What is it, Queen Esther? What is your request? It shall be given you, even to the half of my kingdom. (Est. 5:2–3)

Here we have a glimpse into the incredible relationship between our all-powerful God, who sits on His throne in heaven, and believers who approach His throne from their position on earth to intercede on behalf of His people. (The analogy is an imperfect one, of course, because Artaxerxes, being a pagan king, cannot possibly represent God accurately.)

> We may be reluctant to approach the King of the universe with our puny needs and burdens. But we forget that this King loves us, He has chosen us, He delights in us, and, inexplicably, He has determined to accomplish His purposes on earth in partnership with the prayers of His people.

When we, like Queen Esther, become aware of a need here on earth, we may be reluctant to approach the King of the universe with our puny needs and burdens. But we forget that this King loves us, He has chosen us, He delights in us, and, inexplicably, He has determined to accomplish His purposes on earth in partnership with the prayers of His people. In fact, He is *waiting* for us to come and ask.

We may be fearful to approach One who is so powerful and who could destroy us with a flicker of His eyelids should He so choose. But when we approach His throne, "clothed in His righteousness alone"[4] (even as Esther prepared by putting on her royal robes), wonder of wonders, we win "favor in His sight," He extends His golden scepter toward us, and we are welcomed to draw near and touch the top of the scepter.

Having granted us access into His presence, the King then says to us, "What is your request, my beloved? It shall be given you. Ask, and you will receive."

As the story of Esther progresses, King Artaxerxes asks her the same question three more times (Est. 5:6; 7:2; 9:12), assuring her that there is no limit to his generosity, his desire to bless her, and his ability to fulfill any request she may make—that whatever she asks will be granted.

I often wonder what supernatural acts God would perform

in our world—things He is ready, willing, eager, and able to do—if we would just approach Him and make our requests known. What wonders and blessings does He wish to release that await only the heart cry of one of His subjects down here on earth?

Years ago a friend raised the following question, which has stayed in my mind: If God only did that in my life and the lives of others which I asked Him to do, how much would He do? And how much more might we receive from His hand if only we prayed more?

> Thou art coming to a King—
> Large petitions with thee bring,
> For His grace and pow'r are such,
> None can ever ask too much.[5]

O Lord, make us desperate, and grant us faith and boldness to approach Your throne and make our petitions known, knowing that in so doing we link arms with Omnipotence and become instruments of Your eternal purposes being fulfilled on this earth.

MAKE IT PERSONAL

1. What are the biggest battles you face in your prayer life? What keeps you from approaching His throne to make your petitions?

2. What are you asking God for that only He can do?

3. Read Paul's prayer in Ephesians 3:14–21. Now make this your prayer. Pray these words on behalf of a family member, a friend, or a pastor or Christian leader.

4. If Jesus were to say to you, as He did to the blind beggar in Luke 18:41, "What do you want me to do for you?" how would you answer Him? What would you like to believe God to do in your life? In your family? In your church? In your community and nation?

PART SIX

The Product of a Devotional Life

*Let my beloved come into his garden,
and eat its choicest fruits.*
SONG OF SOLOMON 4:16

Like a watered garden,
Full of fragrance rare,
Ling'ring in Thy presence,
Let my life appear.

E. MAY GRIMES

CHAPTER 12

Cultivating the Garden of the Heart

More than thirty years ago I built (well, I contracted a builder who built!) a home that Robert and I still live in today. When I first purchased the wooded lot, it was covered with tall pine trees as well as lots of brush, tall grass, and weeds. The property was beautifully situated overlooking a river, but for all practical purposes it was useless. I remember when the heavy earthmoving equipment rolled in to clear the land. Many of those trees were cut down to make room for the house. The brush was cleared out, the land was leveled, and the builder began to dig a hole for the basement. The dirt all around that hole quickly got packed down by construction equipment, leaving ground that was hard, dry, and not particularly attractive.

Once the house was up, a landscape architect met with me to propose a plan for the property. He showed me drawings of what he had in mind—lots of trees, plants, shrubs, and ground cover. I couldn't begin to picture what he saw in his mind's eye—I hardly knew a hosta from a hydrangea.

Somewhat apprehensively I signed a contract and said, "Okay, let's do it!"

That fall I paid the landscaping company what seemed to me like a fortune and then sat back to watch. I couldn't believe my eyes! The plants they brought in were tiny, scrawny, and unimpressive, to say the least. Grass seed was planted, but I couldn't see a single blade of grass, much less the verdant carpet I had anticipated. More than once I said to myself, "I paid that much money for *this*?" I had envisioned looking out my window at a lush, colorful visual feast. Instead, there was no color; there was no beauty; and there were large bare spots with no plants at all.

Sensing my lack of enthusiasm, the landscaper urged me to "just wait and see," assuring me that in time I would be pleased with the results. I waited, and I waited, and I waited. When the first Michigan winter hit, things looked even worse. The trees were bare, the ground was bare, and the shrubs looked like sticks poking out of the ground.

The next spring a few trees and shrubs produced nice blossoms. The grass finally looked like grass. But the overall scene was still less than spectacular. And the weeds—oh, the weeds! I had no idea how omnipresent and persistent they could be! I certainly wasn't getting much enjoyment out of this "garden."

I waited some more. We pulled more weeds and applied fertilizer to the beds—and kept waiting. Each year a gardener pruned back the plants, shrubs, and trees. That didn't exactly look like progress to me.

But what I couldn't see was that the sunshine, the rain, the fertilizer, the pruning, even the heavy winter snows were all helping those plants get bigger and stronger and spread their roots deep into the soil. Slowly but surely the ground cover began to take root and spread. Each spring I could see the evidence of new growth at the ends of those evergreen branches. In and among the original plantings, we planted hundreds of daffodil bulbs and lots of brightly colored annuals.

That property is now well established and mature. I can step outdoors any time between May and September and see an array of beautiful flowers and plants.

The daffodils come up first—what a splendid picture they make. By the time they're gone, there are azaleas and astilbes to replace them, followed by splendid daylilies and foxglove, with wild strawberries poking up through the ground cover. What a delight to see butterflies, hummingbirds, cardinals, bluebirds, squirrels, bunnies, and deer making their home in this little earthly paradise.

This outdoor refuge did not spring up overnight. And it did not just "happen." It is the fruit of years of planning, investment, effort, and cultivation, coupled with God's watchful care and provision. Like all gardens, this one requires continual maintenance and care—always keeping an eye out for the disease, rot, moles, and weeds that tend to creep in and take over.

After years of careful oversight (and lots of help from others!), our garden is now fulfilling the purpose for which it was intended. It is a thing of great beauty and provides enjoyment and pleasure to all who visit. It is a peaceful, joyous haven, fragrant, full of new surprises, ever changing—a place where hearts are gladdened and lifted toward the Creator.

> *Your devotional life won't always be easy.... But with time and grace and some perseverance, it can become the kind of lush refuge your heart longs for— a place that bears beautiful fruit.*

And so it is with my daily devotional life—and yours. It won't always be easy, and it won't immediately become a picture-perfect paradise. But with time and grace and some perseverance, it can become the kind of lush refuge our hearts long for—a place that bears beautiful fruit "in its season" (Ps. 1:3).

THE FRUITS OF DEVOTION

What kind of fruit will a daily devotional life yield fruit in our lives? One of the sweetest is an ever-deepening *unity and intimacy with the Father*. Sadly, many believers never enter into the joy and fullness of this life, which takes time and care to cultivate.

The Old Testament Jews were redeemed by God out of Egypt. They were His treasured possession. God spoke to them, but they always had to keep a safe distance, not daring to go near the mountain lest they should die from the glory of His presence. On one occasion, God invited Moses and Aaron and Nadab and Abihu, along with seventy elders of Israel, to come up the mountain to "worship from afar" (Ex. 24:1). Scripture says that those few chosen men "beheld God, and ate and drank" (Ex. 24:11). Together, they partook of a covenant meal, foreshadowing the Lord's Supper that New Testament believers would share with Jesus. However, Moses enjoyed an intimacy with God that was not experienced by anyone else. To Moses alone was granted the privilege of approaching the Lord and speaking with Him "face to face, as a man speaks with his friend" (Ex. 33:11).

In the New Testament, Jesus selected twelve men to be with Him, learn from Him, and walk with Him. Each of these men saw the same miracles, listened to the same messages, shared in the same experiences with the Master. But three of them—Peter, James, and John—formed an "inner circle"; their friendship with Jesus went a level deeper than the others. Of those three John, who identified himself as "the disciple whom Jesus loved," enjoyed an intimacy with Jesus that surpassed that of all others. John 21:20 even says he "leaned back against Jesus" at the last Passover meal they shared.

Those believers who are willing to come apart from the clamor and demands of each day's activity in order to sit at the feet of Jesus and listen to His heart are the ones who will be blessed with intimacy beyond that which most will ever know. It is there, in that quiet time and place, that the words of the old hymn take on new meaning:

> He walks with me, and He talks with me,
>   And He tells me I am His own,
> And the joy we share as we tarry there
>   None other has ever known.[1]

The fruit of a devotional life will also be manifested in *an ordered, peaceful life*. As part of the survey I conducted on this topic, I asked women, "What are the benefits and blessings you have experienced as a result of your devotional life?" By far, the most frequent response was "peace." Their experience seemed to echo that of S. D. Gordon, who wrote,

> Prayer wonderfully clears the vision; steadies the nerves; defines duty; stiffens the purpose; sweetens and strengthens the spirit.[2]

Some time ago I received a call from the leader of a large Christian organization—an older man of God whose walk I greatly respect. He's always been a busy man, but as he's gotten older he's been led to place a much higher priority on his personal devotional life. When I shared with him that I was writing this book, he said this to me:

> Without any question, these past ten years, since I have been disciplined in this area, have been the greatest, the most fruitful, and the most peaceful years of my life. There has been the sense of God orchestrating my days and of the oil of the Spirit in the machinery of my life since I began to spend unhurried time with the Lord.

Time spent alone with Jesus each day will order our hearts and grant a sense of direction, enabling us to live purposeful, useful lives directed by the power of the Holy Spirit, rather than being driven by the expectations and demands of others. It will also—eventually—enable us to touch the lives of others in a powerful way.

I love F. W. Farrar's description of this sweet fruit borne of his mother's daily time with the Lord:

> My mother's habit was every day, immediately after breakfast, to withdraw for an hour to her own room, and to spend that hour in reading the Bible, in meditation and prayer. From that hour, as from a pure fountain, she drew the strength and sweetness which enabled her to fulfill all her duties, and to remain unruffled by the worries and pettinesses which are so often the trial of narrow neighborhoods.
>
> As I think of her life, and all it had to bear, I see the absolute triumph of Christian grace in the lovely ideal of a Christian lady. I never saw her temper disturbed; I never heard her speak one word of anger ... or of idle gossip; I never observed in her any sign

of a single sentiment unbecoming to a soul which had drunk of the river of the water of life, and which had fed upon manna in the barren wilderness.[3]

In his book *How to Worship Jesus Christ*, Joseph Carroll tells of another mother whose spirit was made fruitful by her life of devotion and communion with the Lord Jesus:

> I have lived in literally scores of homes in the forty years of my ministry. On one occasion, I lived in the home of a woman who had seven children and a very unsympathetic husband. She had lost two other children at birth. Though she had a large home to care for and attended the family business in her spare time, I never saw her disturbed once. There was always the fragrance of Christ about her life, and I marveled at it.
>
> While staying in her home during a conference, one morning about five o'clock I noticed light filtering in past the door; so I opened it very quietly and saw this woman kneeling by her piano. I quietly closed the door. The next morning the same thing happened, and the next morning the same thing again.
>
> So, I asked her, "What time do you rise to seek the Lord?"
>
> She replied, "Oh, that is not my decision. I made a choice long ago that when He wanted to have fellowship with me I was available. There are times when He calls me at five; there are times when He calls me at six. And on occasion, He will call about two o'clock in the morning, I think, just to test me." Always she would get up, go to her piano stool, and worship her Lord.
>
> I asked, "How long do you stay?"
>
> "Oh, that is up to Him. When He tells me to go

back to bed, I go back. If He doesn't want me to sleep, I simply stay up."

She was the epitome of serenity. She had made a choice, a choice that was not easy for her to make, for God had to take an idol out of her life before she made it; but when He took that idol, she was Christ's and Christ's alone.[4]

As the example of these two mothers shows, those who spend much time alone with Jesus have a profound *influence on others* (though they themselves are seldom conscious of that influence). You may have thought that if you were to spend quality time each day with the Lord, you would not have time to meet the needs of your family and others. To the contrary, those who have been much with God touch others' lives with the power and glory of God.

After Moses had been with God, his face radiated the reflected glory of God (Ex. 34:29), and the Israelites were moved to worship (33:7–11). Do your countenance and spirit reveal the glory of God to your family and acquaintances and move them to worship God?

And what about the impact of your words? Isaiah 50:4–5 suggests that those whose ears are open to listen to God will have a

> ... well-instructed tongue,
> to know the word that sustains the weary.

When people are emotionally or spiritually drained, do they know that they can come to you and expect to receive wise, encouraging words from the Lord to refresh their spirit?

The Gospels indicate, remember, that Jesus' effectiveness at ministering to the needs of others was born out of His times of communion with His Father:

> He would withdraw to desolate places and pray....
> And the power of the Lord was with him to heal.
> (Luke 5:16–17)

In fact, whenever Jesus withdrew from the crowds for a season to pray, the crowds were drawn to Him like a magnet, for they saw in Him the likeness of His Father:

> He went up on the mountain to pray....The people immediately recognized him and ran about the whole region and began to bring the sick people on their beds to wherever they heard he was....And as many as touched [him] were made well. (Mark 6:46, 55–56)

Are needy people drawn to you, as they were to Jesus, and when they come, does the power of the Holy Spirit flow through you to meet those needs?

Nowhere will the influence of intimate communion with God be more keenly felt than in our own homes and among those who know us best. The following testimony was written by the husband of one of my prayer partners. It illustrates the powerful way in which the sweet fruit of a woman's walk with God can draw her family to hunger for a more intimate relationship with the Lord:

> *Nowhere will the influence of intimate communion with God be more keenly felt than in our own homes and among those who know us best.*

> One of my friends sometimes teases me by reminding me that I married "way over my head." I do have to admit that I often wonder why God would bless me by giving me the mate that He did. My wife is kind, fun-loving, hospitable, and generous. She doesn't grumble about what we don't have and

expresses genuine appreciation for what we do.

There is one thing, however, that stands head and shoulders above all her precious qualities—she walks intimately with God. She listens to what He says, and then she does it. That's not to say that she doesn't struggle, but when she does, she doesn't blame her circumstances or become moody. She asks God to search her heart, and she waits for His answer. I, on the other hand, have often resisted God, languishing in stubbornness, rebellion, and pride. And I'm not fully out of their grip yet. But my life did begin to change a few years ago. Much of that change, my turning to God, came as the result of my wife's consistent, faithful example of godliness.

There is a reason for my wife being the kind of Christian that she is. One of the landmarks that she points to in her life is a time when, during a week of summer youth camp, the speaker encouraged everyone to commit to read their Bible every day for one year. To her, a commitment was a commitment; if she made the promise she was bound by her word to keep it. So when she made that commitment to read her Bible every day for a year, she meant business.

My wife was in junior high school then. As I write this testimony, we have been married for nearly sixteen years, and I have never known her to miss a single day in having her quiet time. Not one.

I'm not saying these things to put my wife on a pedestal. My point is that faithfully taking a few minutes out of each day to meet alone with God in His Word and prayer has formed her into a godly woman. It is her life that "won" me (1 Peter 3:1). If she had nagged me about certain things, or manipulated, or ridiculed, she would only have succeeded in driving me away from wanting to grow in Christ. Instead, she lived a very real life of simple faith and devotion to Christ. And it made me thirsty for what she had.

We have children now. By God's grace they are growing up with an understanding that having personal devotions is a normal part of the daily routine. The older ones have already begun to have their own quiet time. Much like my wife's example to me, we didn't instruct or require this of our children. They've simply seen Mom and Dad reading their Bibles and praying, and they want to do the same.

God's Word has been like a medicine to reduce my anger, worry, and impatience. It has acted as a map in helping our family make decisions or reroute our ill-advised plans. It has provided light to reveal snares that were sometimes hiding in the shadows. God's Word has become for us a thing we simply could not do without.

I thank God for a youth speaker who encouraged a group of junior-high campers to read their Bibles. And I thank God for a young woman who made that commitment and kept it. I can't describe what a blessing it is to be married to a woman who lives and thinks biblically. When we are discussing any issue, whether a hard or not-so-difficult one, I know I'm talking to someone who has been with Jesus! That means a lot to this husband!

MY LIFE—A GARDEN FOR HIM

In the first section of this book, we were introduced to the beautiful young bride of the Song of Solomon. You recall that the king in that amazing love story does not select his bride from among the most eligible women of the capital city, but rather chooses a plain, ordinary country girl who is "burned out" from working in her family's vineyard. He takes her back to the palace and invites her to come into his chamber (Song 1:4). In that intimate, quiet place he lavishes his love upon her. And as she partakes of his fruit, she is restored:

> With great delight I sat in his shadow,
> and his fruit was sweet to my taste.
> He brought me to the banqueting house,
> and his banner over me was love. (2:3–4)

The Song of Solomon is the story of the growing intimacy shared by the royal couple. It depicts the cultivation of a pure, rich love—the intertwining of two lives to become one. As the bride receives the tender words and touch of her beloved and as she responds to his initiative, she is transformed—transformed by grace, transformed by love.

The once common peasant girl becomes a lovely, gracious queen. The girl who was once tired of living now has a purpose for living. The young woman who once resented having to work in the vineyard is now eager to go out among the vines and serve with her beloved (7:11–12). The woman who was once a nobody now brings joy and fullness to the other women of the city as she introduces them to her beloved.

This transformation does not just happen. It takes place in the context of a relationship, and that relationship requires constant attention and care. But there is an ultimate purpose that makes all the investment of time and effort worthwhile. What is that purpose? To bring delight and pleasure to the beloved.

As their love matures, the beloved likens his bride's heart to a garden—a trysting place where he finds great joy and satisfaction. He describes the paradise that he finds in that exclusive place set apart for him:

> A garden locked is my sister, my bride,
>   a spring locked, a fountain sealed.
> Your shoots are an orchard of pomegranates
>   with all choicest fruits . . .
> a garden fountain, a well of living water,
>   and flowing streams from Lebanon. (4:12–13, 15)

The bride responds by affirming that her sole desire is that her garden would bring pleasure to her beloved. She welcomes whatever is required—the cold, biting north winds or the warm, balmy south winds—to cultivate a place of beauty, fragrance, and delight for him:

> Awake, O north wind,
>   and come, O south wind!
> Blow upon my garden,
>   let its spices flow.
> Let my beloved come into his garden,
>   and eat his pleasant fruits. (4:16)

Note that by the end of that passage, the garden that was once hers is now his. The fragrance of that garden is for him. All the fruit of the garden is his. All that she is and all that she has is his. It is all for him,

> for you created all things,
> and by your will they existed and were created.
> (Rev. 4:11)

And so, dear friend, your Beloved, the One who has chosen and redeemed you to be His own, longs to find refuge and delight in the garden of your own heart, which you cultivate in your daily devotional life.

As you walk in union and communion with Him, a sweet fragrance will be released—the aroma of praise, worship, prayer, faith, grace, humility, and more. The time you spend with Him will bear fruit in your life. The result is beauty that blesses you and the others in your life.

But that blessing is simply incidental. It is a side blessing.

Because the beauty that you cultivate as you tend your devotional garden is, ultimately, all for the Beloved.

MAKE IT PERSONAL

1. Write a love letter to Jesus. Thank Him for how He brought you to Himself and for the difference His love has made in your life. Express to Him your desire for your life to be a "garden" that brings pleasure to Him.

2. Take time to think through and record two or three of the most important things God has taught you through your reading of this book. (You may wish to refresh your memory by paging back through the book or reviewing the "Make It Personal" sections.)

3. Go back and review your answer to the first question on page 33. How has the quality of your personal devotional life changed since you began reading this book?

4. What further changes would you like to see take place in your devotional life in the days ahead?

Where to from Here? A 30-Day Challenge

Whenever I've broached this topic, I've been encouraged to discover how many believers are hungry for a more consistent, meaningful devotional life. I hope that has been your experience as you've read this book. But I've also seen that most people need a jump-start to help them develop the habit of carving out time in their day to spend alone with the Lord.

One of the most practical tools I've found to accomplish that is a simple "30-Day Challenge." Rather than asking people to make a lifetime commitment to have a daily quiet time (a commitment they likely won't keep for very long), I've challenged them to get started by making a commitment to *spend some time alone with God in His Word and prayer, every day, for the next thirty days.*

I've extended this challenge to thousands of women, and have been thrilled to see how God has used this commitment to make a world of difference in the lives of tired, needy believers who want to know God in a more intimate way.

Here are some of the kinds of responses I've received from those who have taken the 30-Day Challenge:

A truly phenomenal experience . . .

My life has been beautifully transformed . . .

When I started, fifteen minutes seemed too long, but now two hours isn't long enough! . . .

It's been more than thirty days, and I don't want to stop! . . .

I've been revived! . . .

Before reading this book, the whole idea of a daily devotional life may have been new to you. Or you may have started—and quit—and perhaps started again, only to quit again—maybe many times. Or you may already be enjoying a consistent time alone with God each day. Wherever you are, I want to encourage you to go further . . . to pursue a deeper relationship with God.

Over the years, any time I've spoken on the devotional life, I've closed my message by asking this question: "How many of you would be honest enough to admit that you do *not* currently have a consistent personal devotional life?" I've asked this question scores of times—with groups of lay people, Bible study leaders, and full-time Christian workers. And invariably, 80 to 90 percent of those in the room raise their hand, acknowledging that they are not currently having a regular quiet time.

I have followed that question by inviting people to take the 30-Day Challenge. What a joy it has been to see many thousands of people stand to their feet, signifying their commitment to *spend some time alone with the Lord each day—for the next thirty days.*

A PERSONAL INVITATION

If you've not been enjoying a consistent devotional time with the Lord, the 30-Day Challenge may be just the place for you to start—or to get started again.

You may be wondering how you can possibly add "one more thing" to your already over-crowded schedule. Let me assure you that if you will make knowing God the number one priority of your day, He will show you how to fit everything into your day that is on *His* "to-do" list for you.

Setting aside time alone with the Lord each day has become an absolute necessity for me; there is no richer blessing in my life. That doesn't mean it's always easy—as I've shared, virtually every day I deal with distractions, excuses, and misplaced priorities that would keep me from the "one thing" that matters most. But I've determined that this is a battle worth waging, because I know I cannot be the woman God made me to be—nor can *you*—apart from time spent each day in His presence.

That's why I want to encourage you to take a first step with this 30-Day Challenge. If that is your desire, I'd invite you to sign below as an expression of your commitment to the Lord.

By God's grace, out of a desire to know Him more intimately, I purpose to spend some time alone with the Lord in the Word and in prayer, every day for the next thirty days.

Signed _____

Date _____

Once you've made this commitment, expect that some days you may not have the desire to keep it. Remember that as you choose to feed your soul, your spiritual hunger will grow. Some days you may not seem to be able to find the time to follow through. But if you miss a day, *don't give up!* Simply determine by God's grace to press on. Also, consider reaching out to a friend letting them know that you have committed to this step in developing a daily devotional time and ask them to pray for you. Telling someone else about your commitment can help provide additional accountability and encouragement to see it through.

My prayer is that the 30-Day Challenge will lead to a lifelong pattern and priority of seeking Him every day for the rest of your life and that you will experience the incredible blessings found in knowing Christ, the living Word, and becoming more like Him, until that Day when faith becomes sight and we are forever in His presence.

APPENDIX:

Recommended Devotional Books

The following list is a sampling of many resources that have enriched my daily devotional times over the years. Some of them are classics and in the public domain, which means that you may find multiple publishers or editions from them. Older copies may still be available from online dealers, and the text of some classics may be downloadable as PDFs online. These older gems are definitely worth a little effort to locate.

Alcorn, Randy. *Ninety Days of God's Goodness: Daily Reflections That Shine Light on Personal Darkness.* Multnomah, 2011.

Arnold, Duane W. H., comp. and trans. *Martyrs' Prayers: Seeking God in the Midst of Suffering.* 3rd ed. Reader Hill, 2018.
Note: You may also be able to find the earlier editions of this book: *Prayers of the Martyrs* (Zondervan, 1991) and *Beyond Belief* (Zondervan, 2002).

Bennett, Arthur, ed. *The Valley of Vision*. The Banner of Truth Trust, 1975.

Bonar, Andrew A. *Heavenly Springs*. The Banner of Truth Trust, 1986.

Carson, D. A. *For the Love of God: A Daily Companion for Discovering the Riches of God's Word*. 2 vols. Crossway, 1998–99. Note: This two-volume devotional offers reflections based on the classic M'Cheyne Bible reading plan that takes readers through the New Testament and Psalms twice a year and through the rest of the Old Testament once each year.

Cowman, L. B. (Mrs. Charles E. Cowman), comp. *Streams in the Desert*. Zondervan, 1996 (orig. pub. 1925 by Cowman Publications).

Elliot, Elisabeth. *Keep a Quiet Heart*. Fleming H. Revell, 2004.

Elliot, Elisabeth. *A Lamp unto My Feet: The Bible's Light for Your Daily Walk*. Regal, 2004.

Gurnall, William. *The Christian in Complete Armour*. Reprint edition. Hendrickson, 2010.

Gurnall, William. *Gleanings from William Gurnall*. Edited by Hamilton Smith. Soli Deo Gloria, 1996.

Kelderman, Donna, comp. *Seasons of the Heart: A Year of Devotions from One Generation of Women to Another*. Reformation Heritage, 2013.

Piper, John. *A Godward Life: Savoring the Supremacy of God in All of Life*. Revised edition. Multnomah, 2015.

Spurgeon, C. H. *The Cheque Book of the Bank of Faith: Daily Readings by C. H. Spurgeon*. Rev. ed. Christian Heritage, 2014.

Watson, Thomas. *Gleanings from Thomas Watson*. Edited by Hamilton Smith. Soli Deo Gloria, 1995.

Notes

Dedication
1. Song of Solomon 5:10, 16 and 8:13 (NKJV).

From My Heart to Yours
1. This term comes from a poem of the same name by the English poet Francis Thompson (1859–1907), which depicts God's relentlessly pursuing love.

Part One: The Priority of a Devotional Life
Epigraph: Andrew Murray, *The Secret of Fellowship* (CLC Publications, 2019), Introduction.

Chapter 2: Made for Intimacy
1. Charles F. Pfeiffer and Everett F. Harrison, eds., *The Wycliffe Bible Commentary* (Moody, 1990), 1047.

Part Two: The Purpose of a Devotional Life
Epigraph: Andrew Murray, *The Secret of Fellowship* (CLC Publications, 2019), Introduction.

Chapter 3: The Inner Life
1. Mary A. Lathbury (1841–1913), "Break Thou the Bread of Life," *Baptist Hymnal 2008*, #407, accessed on Hymnary.org, https://hymnary.org/hymn/BH2008/407, emphasis added.
2. Warren Patrick Baker, *The Complete Word Study Old Testament*, Word Study Series (AMG, 1994), 2372.

Chapter 4: The Outer Walk
1. Joseph M. Scriven (1819–1896), "What a Friend We Have in Jesus," *Baptist Hymnal 2008*, #154, accessed on Hymnary.org, https://hymnary.org/hymn/BH2008/154.
2. Andrew Murray, *With Christ in the School of Prayer*, 139.
3. "Lexicon: Strong's G3339 metamorphoó," *Blue Letter Bible*, https://www.blueletterbible.org/lang/lexicon/lexicon.cfm?t=esv&strongs=g3339.
4. "Lexicon: Strong's G3345 metaschēmatizō," *Blue Letter Bible*, https://www.blueletterbible.org/lang/lexicon/lexicon.cfm?t=ESV&strongs=g3345.
5. William D. Longstaff (1822–1894), "Take Time to Be Holy," *Hymnal for Worship and Celebration*, #440, accessed on Hymnary.org, https://hymnary.org/hymn/HWC1986/441.

Part Three: The Pattern of a Devotional Life
Epigraph: L. B. Cowman (Mrs. Charles E. Cowman), comp., *Streams in the Desert*, March 2, Crosswalk.com, https://www.crosswalk.com/devotionals/desert/streams-in-the-desert-march-2nd.html.

Chapter 5: Getting Started
1. Donald S. Whitney, *Spiritual Disciplines for the Christian Life*, rev. ed. (Navpress, 2015), 113.
2. John Blanchard, *How to Enjoy Your Bible* (Evangelical, 1984), 104, quoted in Whitney, *Spiritual Disciplines*, 28.
3. This quote is attributed to J. Hudson Taylor.
4. Charles H. Spurgeon, "Morning and Evening Songs," Sermon No. 1138, delivered at the Metropoliltan Tabernacle, Newington, UK, from *Metropolitan Tabernacle Pulpit Volume 19* (1873), Spurgeon Gems (website),https://www.spurgeongems.org/chsbm19.pdf.
5. Thomas Watson, *Gleanings from Thomas Watson*, comp. Hamilton Smith (Soli Deo Gloria, 1995), 105–106.
6. Ralph Spaulding Cushman, "The Secret," *Spiritual Hilltops* (Abingdon-Cokesbury, 1932), cited in James Dalton Morrison, ed., *Masterpieces of Religious Verse* (Harper and Brothers, 1948), 408–409. Available online at https://archive.org/details/masterpiecesofre002909mbp/page/n425.
7. L. B. Cowman, *Streams in the Desert*, December 4, Crosswalk.com, https://www.crosswalk.com/devotionals/desert/streams-in-the-desert-december-4th.html.

Part Four: The Problems of a Devotional Life
Epigraph: John Donne, "Sermon LXXX," preached at the Funerals of Sir William Cokayne, Knt. Alderman of London, December 12, 1626, from *The Works of John Donne Volume 3*, Bible Study Tools, https://www.biblestudytools.com/classics/the-works-of-john-donne-vol-3/sermon-lxxx.html.

Chapter 6: "The Hard Thing for Me Is . . ."
1. William Gurnall, *Gleanings from William Gurnall*, comp. Hamilton Smith (Soli Deo Gloria Publications, 1996), 104–105.
2. Lewis Bayly, *The Practice of Piety: Directing a Christian to Walk, That He May Please God* (Soli Deo Gloria Publications, 1995), 107.
3. John Piper (@JohnPiper), "One of the great uses of Twitter and Facebook will be to prove at the Last Day that prayeressness was not from lack of time," Twitter, October 20, 2009, 5:02pm, https://x.com/JohnPiper/status/5027319857.
4. D. Martyn Lloyd-Jones, *God's Ultimate Purpose: An Exposition of Ephesians 1:1 to 23* (Baker, 1995), 330.
5. John Donne, "Sermon LXXX," preached at the Funerals of Sir William Cokayne, Knt. Alderman of London, December 12, 1626, from *The Works of John Donne Volume 3*, on Bible Study Tools, https://www.biblestudytools.com/classics/the-works-of-john-donne-vol-3/sermon-lxxx.html.
6. C. I. Scofield, *Scofield Reference Notes (1917 Edition), Genesis 17:1*, Bible Study Tools, https://www.biblestudytools.com/commentaries/scofield-reference-notes/genesis/genesis-17.html. See also Charles H. Spurgeon, "Consecration to God—Illustrated

APPENDIX: RECOMMENDED DEVOTIONAL BOOKS

by Abraham's Circumcision," Sermon No. 845, from *Metropolitan Tabernacle Pulpit Volume 14 (1868)*, delivered December 13, 1868 at the Metropolitan Tabernacle, Newington, UK, from *Metropolitan Tabernacle Pulpit Volume 14*, Spurgeon Gems (website), https://www.spurgeongems.org/chsbm14.pdf.

7. Charles H. Spurgeon, *The Salt-Cellars: Being a Collection of Proverbs Together with Homely Notes Theron, Vol. 1—A to L* (Passmore and Alabaster, 1889), 58. Note: this quote is one of Spurgeon's "homely notes" in his collected proverbs and is found, strangely, in the "A" section of the book.

Part Five: The Practice of a Devotional Life

Epigraph: Oswald J. Smith, *The Man God Uses* (Welch, 1984), 91.

Part Five: Section One: Receiving His Word

Epigraph: George Müller, in *Spiritual Secrets of George Müller*, ed. Roger Steer (Harold Shaw, 1985), 60–61.

Chapter 7: The Wonder of the Word

1. This story is recounted in Mary Emily Rope, *Mary Jones and Her Bible, Classic Stories, repr. ed.* (Christian Focus/CF4Kids, 2015, orig. pub. 1882). Charles Thomas's encounter with Mary Jones deeply impressed him and led to the establishment in 1804 of the British and Foreign Bible Society, a society dedicated to publishing and distributing the Word of God throughout the world.

2. In Kevin Miller, ed., *Christian History*, vol. 11, no. 2 (1992), 2–51, quoted by Amanda Duke, "Martin Luther: The Man, the Myth, the Legend," LITS blog, Asbury Seminary Library Resources, October 30, 2017, https://guides.asburyseminary.edu/blog/martin-luther-the-man-the-myth-the-legend.33

3. Augustine, *The City of God*, 3.8–11, tr. David S. Wiesten (Harvard University Press, 1968), quoted in Steven Lawson, *The Moment of Truth* (Reformation Trust/Ligonier, 2018), 35. This quote by Augustine was famously repeated by John Calvin and later reiterated by B. B. Warfield.

4. John Burton (1773–1822), "Holy Bible, Book Divine," *Baptist Hymnal 2008*, #345, accessed at Hymnary.org, https://hymnary.org/hymn/BH2008/345.

5. Lewis Bayly, *The Practice of Piety: Directing a Christian How to Walk, That He May Please God*, ed. Anthony Uyl (Devoted Publishing, 2018, orig. pub. 1842), 81.

6. Emily May Grimes [Crawford] (1868–1927), "The Quiet Hour," *The Cyber Hymnal* (http://www.hymntime.com/tch), #5720, accessed on Hymnary.org, https://hymnary.org/hymn/CYBER/5720.

7. Clara H. Scott (1841–1897), "Open My Eyes, That I May See," *Baptist Hymnal 2008*, #443, accessed on Hymnary.org, https://hymnary.org/hymn/BH2008/443.

Chapter 8: Getting into the Word

1. Attributed to David F. Nygren in Bill Bradfield, ed., *On Reading the Bible: Thoughts and Reflections of Over 500 Men and Women, from St. Augustine to Oprah Winfrey* (Dover, 2005), 90.

2. Oswald Chambers, *Approved unto God*, in *The Complete Works of Oswald Chambers* (Discovery House, 2000, orig. pub. 1936), 5, accessed online at https://vdocuments.mx/complete-works-oswald-chambers-fv162.html.

3. William Gurnall, *Gleanings from William Gurnall*, comp. Hamilton Smith (Soli Deo Gloria Publications, 1996), 104–105.

4. Frances Ridley Havergal (1836–1879), "Master Speak! Thy Servant Heareth," *The Cyber Hymnal* (http://www.hymntime.com/tch), #4174, accessed on Hymnary.org, https://hymnary.org/hymn/CYBER/4174.

5. Thomas Watson in *Gleanings from Thomas Watson*, comp. Hamilton Smith (Soli Deo Gloria Publications, 1995), 106, 112.

6. Donald S. Whitney, *Spiritual Disciplines for the Christian Life*, rev. ed. (Navpress, 2015), 38.

7. Darlene Deibler Rose, *Evidence Not Seen* (Harper & Row, 1988), 143.

8. John Bunyan, "The Conclusion," *Grace Abounding to the Chief of Sinners, in a Faithful Acccount of the Life and Death of John Bunyan*, in *The Works of That Eminent Servant of Christ, John Bunyan*, vol. 1 (James Locken, 1832), 43.

9. Oswald Chambers, *Disciples Indeed*, in *Our Brilliant Heritage / If You Will Be Perfect / Disciples Indeed: The Inheritance of God's Transforming Mind and Heart* (Discovery House, 2015, *Disciples Indeed* orig. pub 1955), chapter entitled "The Bible."

10. Richard Cecil, *The Remains of the Rev. Richard Cecil* (Eliot Stock, 1876), 16.

11. Bibleplan.org is an excellent place to start in locating some of these.

12. The lyrics to this beloved gospel song were penned by Florence Horton and first published in 1906.

13. Oswald Chambers, *As He Walked*, in *Our Brilliant Heritage / If You Will Be Perfect / Disciples Indeed: The Inheritance of God's Transforming Mind and Heart* (Discovery House, 2015, *As He Walked* orig. pub. 1930), chapter/section entitled "Pull Yourself Together . . . By the Habit of Constantly Remembering."

Chapter 9: Getting the Word into You

1. Charles H. Spurgeon, "The Swiftly Running Word," Sermon No. 1607, delivered July 3, 1881 at the Metropolitan Tabernacle, Newington, UK, from *Metropolitan Tabernacle Pulpit Volume 27* (1881), Spurgeon Gems (website), https://www.spurgeongems.org/chsbm27.pdf.

2. *CSB Notetaking Bible* (Holman Bible Publishers, 2017). The *Revive Our Hearts* edition of the *Notetaking Bible* (2025) includes suggestions for Bible journaling as well as 150 prayers based on my personal meditation on Scripture.

3. Martin Luther, quoted in *The Westminister Collection of Christian Quotations*, ed. Martin H. MansSer (Westminster John Knox, 2001), 363.

4. Noah Webster's *Dictionary of the American Language* is available online at http://webstersdictionary1828.com/. If you prefer to own your own hardcover, you can purchase either a "compact edition" or a full facsimile edition of the first edition, published by the Foundation for American Christian Education. At the time of this publication, both were available from Amazon.com, and the facsimile edition can be purchased directly from F.A.C.E. at https://face.net/noah-websters-1828-dictionary/.

5. A useful resource for comparing translations of specific phrases is BibleGateway.com.

6. If you're not familiar with the Hebrew and Greek dictionaries at the back of *Strong's*, ask your pastor or another experienced student of the Word to show you how to use them.

APPENDIX: RECOMMENDED DEVOTIONAL BOOKS

7. If you are using the *English Standard Version* as your basic study Bible, try *The ESV Exhaustive Concordance*, comp. Drayton C. Benner (Crossway, 2018). Similarly, the *Zondervan NASB Exhaustive Concordance*, ed. Reuben A. Olsen, Robert L. Thomas, et al. (Zondervan, 2000), will be useful if you use the NASB. You can also find these resources online at study sites such as Blue Letter Bible (blueletterbible.org) and Bible Hub (biblehub.com).

8. A few commentaries and study Bibles I have found helpful: *The ESV Study Bible* (Crossway); *The MacArthur Study Bible* (Crossway, Thomas Nelson); *The Bible Knowledge Commentary*, ed. John F. Walvoord and Roy B. Zuck (Victor Books); and *The Wycliffe Bible Commentary*, ed. Charles F. Pfeiffer and Everett F. Harrison (Moody). A useful online resource is "The Enduring Word Commentary" with study notes and teaching videos by Pastor David Guzik: www.EnduringWord.com.

9. Quoted in "Rodney 'Gipsy' Smith Quotes," AZQuotes, https://www.azquotes.com/author/50640-Rodney_Gipsy_Smith.

10. Charles H. Spurgeon, "Prayer 22: The Presence of God," *C. H. Spurgeon's Prayers*, Spurgeon Gems (website), http://www.spurgeongems.org/chs_prayers.htm.

Part Five: Section Two: Responding to His Word
Epigraph: George Müller, in *Spiritual Secrets of George Müller*, ed. Roger Steer (Harold Shaw, 1985), 61.

Chapter 10: The Perfume of Praise

1. Many commentators believe that Mary of Bethany is the woman referred to in Matthew 26:6–13, Mark 14:3–9, and John 12:1–8. Others believe that the accounts in Matthew and Mark refer to a different woman. A case can be made for either conclusion. I have taken the first position in this chapter. (A similar account found in Luke 7:36–50 clearly refers to a woman other than Mary.)

2. Edward Perronet (1726–1792), "All Hail the Power of Jesus' Name," *Lift Up Your Hearts: Psalms, Hymns, and Spiritual Songs*, ed. Joyce Borger, Martin Tel, John D. Witvliet (Faith Alive Christian Resources, 2013), #601, accessed on Hymnary.org, https://hymnary.org/hymn/LUYH2013/601.

3. "Lexicon: Strong's H1984 halal," Blue Letter Bible, https://www.blueletterbible.org/lang/lexicon/lexicon.cfm?page=2&strongs=h3034&t=esv#lexResults.

4. "Lexicon: Strong's H1288 barak," Blue Letter Bible, https://www.blueletterbible.org/lang/lexicon/lexicon.cfm?page=5&strongs=h1288&t=esv#lexResults.

5. James Montgomery (1771–1854), "Stand Up and Bless the Lord," *Hymnal for Worship and Celebration*, #21, accessed on Hymnary.org, https://hymnary.org/hymn/HWC1986/21.

6. "Lexicon: Strong's H3034 yadah," Blue Letter Bible, https://www.blueletterbible.org/lang/lexicon/lexicon.cfm?page=2&strongs=h3034&t=esv#lexResults.

7. Timothy Dudley-Smith (1926–2024), "Tell Out, My Soul," *Hymnal for Worship and Celebration*, #27, accessed on Hymnary.org, https://hymnary.org/hymn/HWC1986/27. Copyright © 1962 Hope Publishing Co., Carol Stream, IL 60188. All rights reserved. Used by permission.

8. *Strong's Exhaustive Concordance*.

9. Ibid.

10. These seven rules were first included in the 1761 publication *Select Hymns*, a hymnbook for early Methodists. chrome-extension://efaidnbmnnnibpcajpcglclefindmkaj/ https://archives.gcah.org/server/api/core/bitstreams/62c561cb-4aa2-4f3c-973a-6c02975c5bb7/content.

11. Henry F. Lyte (1793–1847), "Praise My Soul the King of Heaven," *Hymnal for Worship and Celebration*, #3, accessed on Hymnary.org, https://hymnary.org/hymn/HWC1986/3.

Chapter 11: The Privilege of Prayer

1. William Gurnall, *Gleanings from William Gurnall*, comp. Hamilton Smith (Soli Deo Gloria Publications, 1996), 104.

2. Andrew Bonar, *Heavenly Springs: Portions for the Sabbaths of a Year* (Titus Books, 2014), chapter 48, Kindle.

3. Ibid., chapter 42.

4. Edward Mote (1797–1874), "My Hope Is Built on Nothing Less," *Evangelical Lutheran Hymnary* (MorningStar, 1996), #197, accessed on Hymnary.org, https://hymnary.org/hymn/ELH1996/197. Note: This phrase from the fourth stanza of the hymn is based on Isaiah 61:10.

5. John Newton (1725–1807), "Come, My Soul, Thy Suit Prepare" *Evangelical Lutheran Hymnary*, #381, accessed on Hymnary.org, https://hymnary.org/hymn/ELH1996/381.

Part Six: The Product of a Devotional Life

Epigraph: Emily May Grimes [Crawford] (1868–1927), "The Quiet Hour," *The Cyber Hymnal* (http://www.hymntime.com/tch), #5720, accessed on Hymnary.org, https://hymnary.org/hymn/CYBER/5720.

Chapter Twelve: Cultivating the Garden of the Heart

1. C. Austin Miles (1868–1946), "In the Garden," *Baptist Hymnal 2008*, #476, accessed on Hymnary.com, https://hymnary.org/hymn/BH2008/476.

2. S. D. Gordon, *Quiet Talks on Prayer, updated and abridged ed.*, Faith Classics (Barbour, 2015), 174.

3. F. W. Farrar, quoted in Cowman, *Streams in the Desert*, September 13, Crosswalk.com, https://www.crosswalk.com/devotionals/desert/streams-in-the-desert-september-13th.html.

4. Joseph S. Carroll, *How to Worship Jesus Christ: Experiencing His Manifest Presence Daily* (Moody Publishers, 2013), 30–31.

Thank You

How grateful I am for each person whose efforts helped make this revised edition possible—chief among them:

The **Moody Publishers** team that first urged me to write this book in 1998 and has partnered with me through the publishing of dozens of books since. What a privilege it has been to magnify and serve our King together.

Anne Christian Buchanan whose considerable editing skills and wisdom were invaluable in a revision process that I managed to spread out over several years.

Erik Wolgemuth, my literary agent who lightens my load with his faithful assistance and encouragement (and his patient, gracious attention to my endless emails) on each publishing project.

Nancy DeMoss Wolgemuth is the founder and lead Bible teacher for *Revive Our Hearts*, a ministry dedicated to calling women to freedom, fullness, and fruitfulness in Christ. Nancy's love for Christ and passion for helping women cultivate a vibrant daily devotional life are evident through her writing, digital, and conference outreaches and her two daily audio teachings—*Revive Our Hearts* and *Seeking Him*. Her books have sold millions of copies and are reaching the hearts of women around the world. Nancy and her husband, Robert, live in Michigan.

Take the Next Step

Draw near to God. Dwell in His Word.
Delight in the journey.

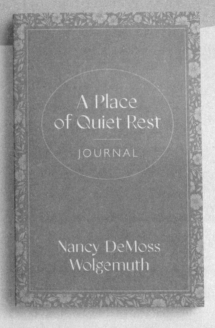

Establish a devotional habit rooted in God's Word with this 30-day companion to *A Place of Quiet Rest*.

"When I started, fifteen minutes seemed too long, but now two hours isn't long enough!"

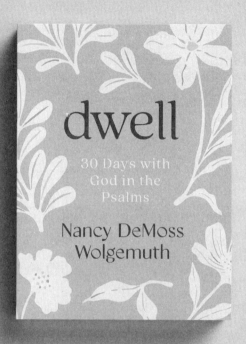

Settle in and savor time with God.

Dwell guides you through thirty selected psalms with rich devotional content and space to reflect and respond as you meditate on His Word each day.

Whether you are just starting your devotional life or ready to go deeper—He will meet you there.

Calling Women to Freedom,
Fullness, and Fruitfulness in Christ

Daily Teaching | Events | Broadcast Media
Resources | Digital Content

For additional teaching from Nancy DeMoss Wolgemuth visit

ReviveOurHearts.com

Your Trustworthy Source for Biblical Truth